THE TAOISM

The

TAOISM
READER

Translated and Edited by
THOMAS CLEARY

SHAMBHALA
Boston & London
2011

Shambhala Publications, Inc.
Horticultural Hall
300 Massachusetts Avenue
Boston, Massachusetts 02115
www.shambhala.com

9 8 7 6 5 4 3 2 1

Printed in Canada

⊛ This edition is printed on acid-free paper that meets the
American National Standards Institute Z39.48 Standard.
♻ This book was printed on 30% recycled paper.
For more information please visit www.shambhala.com
Distributed in the United States by Random House, Inc.,
and in Canada by Random House of Canada Ltd

Library of Congress Cataloging-in-Publication Data

The Taoism reader/translated and edited by Thomas Cleary.
p.   cm.
Includes bibliographical references.
ISBN 978-1-59030-950-6 (pbk.: alk. paper)
1. Taoism—Sacred books—Quotations.
I. Cleary, Thomas F., 1949– II. Title.
BL1900.A1S65 2011
299.5'1482—dc23
2011028691

CONTENTS

Classic Sources

INTRODUCTION

Tao-te Ching

The *Tao-te Ching* is the most widely read of Taoist texts and the most universally accepted by followers of all Taoist orders. It has been dated variously, with estimates generally ranging from around 500 to 300 B.C.E. Although it is conventionally attributed to Lao-tzu, a semilegendary ancestor of Taoism, the *Tao-te Ching* is evidently not an original composition by an individual author, but contains redactions of even more ancient lore. In any case, it is one of the earliest sources of Taoist theory and praxis. The present anthology includes several key selections from the classic illustrating these teachings.

Chuang-tzu

The next great Taoist classic after the *Tao-te Ching* is the equally famous *Chuang-tzu*, or *Book of Master Chuang*, attributed to the philosopher Chuang-tzu, or Chuang Chou (ca. 369–286 B.C.E.). Although it elaborates on many of the ideas of the *Tao-te Ching*, the *Chuang-tzu* is very different in its transmission and manner of presentation. Whereas the former text consists of proverbs and aphorisms, the latter is largely made up of allegorical stories interspersed with philosophical discussions. The *Tao-te Ching*, closely linked to ancient tradition, is attributed to a semilegendary sage and is very difficult to place historically with precision; the *Chuang-tzu*, on the other hand, is attributed to a clearly historical personage, and the marks of its time, during which the chaos and violence of the Warring States era rose inexorably toward a climax, are quite evident in the psychological mood and philosophical attitude of the text.

Huai-nan-tzu

The next great Taoist classic after Chuang-tzu is the *Huai-nan-tzu* (Huainanzi), or "Masters of Huai-nan," composed approximately 150 years later in a very different social and political climate. Centuries of civil war had ended around 200 B.C.E. with the founding of the monumental Han dynasty, which was to rule China for the next four hundred years, with but a brief interruption in the early part of the first century C.E. Although the later impact of Buddhism was so great as to be immeasurable, nevertheless the culture of the Han dynasty left an indelible imprint, exerting a lasting influence on the development of Chinese civilization.

The early emperors of Han adopted a Taoist policy of minimalist government in order to allow the nation and its people to recover from the violence and destruction of the long era of Warring States. China had been united into an empire under the militaristic Ch'in dynasty in the middle of the third century B.C.E.; taking over from the Ch'in, the Han dynasty attempted to restore classical culture, which had been suppressed by the Ch'in government in favor of a mechanical form of legalism. One of the great patrons of this revival was Liu An, a grandson of the founding Han emperor and king of a small feudal domain. Known as the king of Huai-nan after the region where his fief was at one time located, Liu An opened his court to scholars and savants from all over the empire, developing it into a major center of learning and culture.

According to legend, the classic *Huai-nan-tzu* is the product of an inner circle of eight Taoist sages at Liu An's court. This group of wizards is said to have appeared at court when it was already in full bloom as a seat of arts and sciences. Challenged by the king to demonstrate knowledge not already represented at his illustrious court, the eight ancients proceeded to astound him with uncanny displays of occult

powers. Duly humbled, the king of Huai-nan wel-
comed the sages and apprenticed himself to them.
The *Huai-nan-tzu* purports to be records of their talks.

Because of the historical circumstances of its origin, the *Huai-nan-tzu* contains a great deal of material
relating to political science and affairs of state; but it
also synthesizes other aspects of Taoism, including
natural and spiritual sciences. In this respect it is
the richest of the early Taoist classics. The dissemi-
nation of these teachings was inhibited, however, by
two events: the downfall and disappearance of Liu
An, victim of an intrigue; and the official adoption
of a form of Confucianism as the orthodox system of
thought and education throughout the empire. The
brand of Confucianism that won the imperial stamp
of approval was really a hybrid of Confucianism, legalism, and a peculiar cosmology that revived the
ancient doctrine of the divine right of kings and bestowed on it the dignity and authority of natural law.

Thus the liberal, egalitarian idealism of the Taoist
Huai-nan masters was eclipsed by the imperial ide-
ology of political despotism and intellectual con-
formism. Nevertheless, the essential vitality, energy,
and spirit of Taoism remained stored within its own
secret reservoirs in spite of external barriers to its
effective application on a large scale: as the Huai-nan
masters themselves said, "To blame the Way for not

working in a polluted world is like tying a unicorn down from two sides and yet expecting it to run a thousand miles." The teachings of the Huai-nan-tzu may not have had the social and political impact that could have been possible under more favorable conditions, but they retained incalculable value as a basic resource for Taoist principles and practices.

Although the Huai-nan-tzu follows the Tao-te Ching and the Chuang-tzu in its fundamental understanding of human nature and life, because of the historical circumstances of its composition it is more positive and constructive than either of its great predecessors, especially the Chuang-tzu.

Wen-tzu

After the downfall of Liu An, the disappearance of the Huai-nan masters, and the establishment of Confucian orthodoxy in the second century B.C.E., the classical Taoist tradition of the Tao-te Ching, the Chuang-tzu, and the Huai-nan-tzu went underground. There remained considerable private interest in Taoism among the Confucian intelligentsia, but over the course of the Han dynasty their "Taoism" became mixed with superstitions and mechanical thought systems characteristic of hybrid Han Confucianism. Among Taoist purists, it is said that so-called Real

People, or true Taoist adepts, went into hiding during the Han dynasty and did not reemerge for hundreds of years.

The *Wen-tzu* (Wen zi) occupies a unique position in this complex historical context. Its compilation is attributed to a disciple of Lao-tzu, with virtually all of its contents presented as sayings of Lao-tzu himself. Although later Taoist literature includes many texts ascribed to Lao-tzu, they refer to the ancient master by honorific epithets attached to him as the apotheosized founder of Taoism, a transhistorical immortal reappearing in the world from age to age. *Wen-tzu*, on the other hand, uses the names Lao-tzu and Lao Tan, suggesting greater antiquity. This is reinforced by the contents of the work, which follow more closely on the classic tradition than do later texts attributed to the transcendental personalities of the founder. Non-Taoist historical evidence would seem to indicate that the text may have been compiled around 100 B.C.E., not long after the *Huai-nan-tzu*, and later augmented to form an expanded version. Linguistic evidence also suggests an early Han dynasty origin.

The *Wen-tzu* contains many extracts from its predecessors, *Tao-te Ching*, *Chuang-tzu*, and particularly the *Huai-nan-tzu*. In a sense, the *Wen-tzu* may be considered something like an early commentary on these texts, or an attempt to continue the classic tradition after its fall from political grace. In terms of format the *Wen-tzu* follows the *Tao-te Ching*; generally abstract and timeless like its model, the *Wen-tzu* does not include the kind of stories and allusions that make *Chuang-tzu* and *Huai-nan-tzu* extravagantly colorful and difficult to read. It does, nevertheless, contain many images and metaphors that are not found in the earlier texts but are effective in illustrating and vivifying the ancient teachings. Like the *Huai-nan-tzu*, its immediate predecessor, the *Wen-tzu* embraces a wide range of related topics, from physiology and health lore to social and political science.

TAO-TE CHING

Carrying Vitality and Consciousness

Carrying vitality and consciousness,
embracing them as one,
can you keep them from parting?
Concentrating energy,
making it supple,
can you be like an infant?
Purifying hidden perception,
can you make it flawless?
Loving the people, governing the nation,
can you be uncontrived?
As the gate of heaven opens and closes,
can you be impassive?
As understanding reaches everywhere,
can you be innocent?
Producing and developing,
producing without possessing,
doing without presuming,
growing without domineering:
this is called mysterious power.

Colors

Colors blind people's eyes,
sounds deafen their ears;
flavors spoil people's palates,
the chase and the hunt
craze people's minds;
goods hard to get
make people's actions harmful.
Therefore sages work for the core
and not the eyes,
leaving the latter and taking the former.

Attain the Climax of Emptiness

Attain the climax of emptiness,
preserve the utmost quiet:
as myriad things act in concert,
I thereby observe the return.
Things flourish,
then each returns to its root.
Returning to the root is called stillness:
stillness is called return to Life,
return to Life is called the constant;
knowing the constant is called enlightenment.
Acts at random, in ignorance of the constant,
bode ill.
Knowing the constant gives perspective;
this perspective is impartial.
Impartiality is the highest nobility;
the highest nobility is divine,
and the divine is the Way.
This Way is everlasting,
not endangered by physical death.

Knowing the Male

Knowing the male, keep the female;
be humble to the world.
Be humble to the world,
and eternal power never leaves,
returning again to innocence.
Knowing the white, keep the black;
be an examplar for the world.
Be an exemplar for the world,
and eternal power never goes awry,
returning again to infinity.
Knowing the glorious, keep the ignominious;
be open to the world.
Be open to the world,
and eternal power suffices,
returning again to simplicity.
Simplicity is lost to make instruments,
which sages employ as functionaries.
Therefore the great fashioner does no splitting.

The Way Is Always Uncontrived

The Way is always uncontrived,
yet there's nothing it doesn't do.
If lords and monarchs could keep it,
all beings would evolve spontaneously.
When they have evolved and want to act,
I would stabilize them with nameless simplicity.
Even nameless simplicity would not be wanted.
By not wanting, there is calm,
and the world will straighten itself.

Return Is the Movement of the Way

Return is the movement of the Way;
yielding is the function of the Way.
All things in the world are born of being;
being is born of nonbeing.

When the World Has the Way

When the world has the Way,
  running horses are retired to manure the fields.
When the world lacks the Way,
  warhorses are bred in the countryside.
No crime is greater than approving of greed,
  no calamity is greater than discontent,
  no fault is greater than possessiveness.
So the satisfaction of contentment is always
enough.

The World Has a Beginning

The world has a beginning
that is the mother of the world.
Once you've found the mother,
thereby you know the child.
Once you know the child,
you return to keep the mother,
not perishing though the body die.
Close your eyes, shut your doors,
and you do not toil all your life.
Open your eyes, carry out your affairs,
and you are not saved all your life.
Seeing the small is called clarity,
keeping flexible is called strength.
Using the shining radiance,
you return again to the light,
not leaving anything to harm yourself.
This is called entering the eternal.

The Richness of Subliminal Virtue

The richness of subliminal virtue
is comparable to an infant:
poisonous creatures do not sting it,
wild beasts do not claw it,
predatory birds do not grab it.
Its tendons are flexible,
yet its grip is firm.
Even while it knows not
of the mating of male and female,
its genitals get aroused;
this is the epitome of vitality.
It can cry all day without choking or getting hoarse;
this is the epitome of harmony.
Knowing harmony is called constancy,
knowing constancy is called clarity;
enhancing life is called propitious,
the mind mastering energy is called strong.
When beings climax in power, they wane;
this is called being unguided.
The unguided die early.

When People Are Born

When people are born they are supple,
and when they die they are stiff.
When trees are born they are tender,
and when they die they are brittle.
Stiffness is thus a cohort of death,
flexibility is a cohort of life.
So when an army is strong,
it does not prevail.
When a tree is strong,
it is cut for use.
So the stiff and strong are below,
the supple and yielding on top.

CHUANG-TZU

Small fear is fearful, great fear is slow. In action they are like a bolt, an arrow, in terms of their control over judgment. In stillness they are like a prayer, a pledge, in terms of their attachment to victory. They kill like fall and winter, in the sense of daily dissolution. Their addiction to what they do is such as to be irreversible. Their satiation is like a seal, meaning that they deepen with age. The mind drawing near to death cannot bring about a restoration of positivity.

Joy, anger, sadness, happiness, worry, lament, vacillation, fearfulness, volatility, indulgence, licentiousness, pretentiousness—these are like sounds issuing from hollows, or moisture producing mildew. Day and night they interchange before us, yet no one knows where they sprout. Stop, stop! From morning to evening we find them; do they arise from the same source?

If not for other, there is no self. If not for self, nothing is apprehended. This is not remote, but we don't know what constitutes the cause. There seems to be a real director, but we cannot find any trace of it. Its effectiveness is already proven, but we don't see its form. It has sense, but no form.

The whole body is there with all of its members, openings, and organs: with which is the self associated? Do you like any of them? That means you have selfishness therein. Then do all sometimes act as servants? As servants, are they incapable of taking care of one another? Do they alternate as ruler and subject? Evidently there is a real ruler existing therein: the matter of whether or not we gain a sense of it does not increase or decrease its reality.

Once we have taken on a definite form, we do not lose it until death. We oppose things, yet also follow them; we violate things, yet also submit to them: that activity is all like a galloping horse that no one can stop. Isn't it pitiful? We work all our lives without seeing it accomplish anything. We wearily work to exhaustion, without even knowing what it all goes back to. How can we not be sad about this? People may say at least it isn't death, but what help is that? As the physical constitution changes, so does the mind; how can this not be considered a great sorrow?

Once a butcher was cutting up an ox for a king. As he felt with his hand, leaned in with his shoulder, stepped in and bent a knee to it, the carcass fell apart with a peculiar sound as he played his cleaver.

The king, expressing admiration, said to the butcher, "Good! It seems that this is the consummation of technique."

The butcher put down his cleaver and replied, "What I like is the Way, which is more advanced than technique. But I will present something of technique.

"When I first began to cut up oxen, all I saw was an ox. Even after three years I still had not seen a whole ox. Now I meet it with spirit rather than look at it with my eyes.

"When sensory knowledge stops, then the spirit is ready to act. Going by the natural pattern, I separate the joints, following the main apertures, according to the nature of its formation. I have never even cut into a mass of gristle, much less a large bone.

"A good butcher changes cleavers every year because of damage, a mediocre butcher changes cleavers every month because of breakage. I've had this cleaver for nineteen years now, and it has cut up thousands of oxen; yet its blade is as though it had newly come from the whetstone."

Yen Hui asked Confucius, "May I hear about mental fasting?"

Confucius replied, "You unify your will: hear with the mind instead of the ears; hear with the energy instead of the mind. Hearing stops at the ears, the mind stops at contact, but energy is that which is empty and responsive to others. The Way gathers in emptiness; emptiness is mental fasting."

Yen Hui said, "The reason I haven't been able to master this is because I consider myself really me. If I could master this, 'I' would not exist. Could that be called emptiness?"

Confucius said, "That's all there is to it. I tell you, you can go into the political arena without being moved by repute. If you are heard, then speak; if not, then stop. Let there be no dogma, no drastic measures: remain consistent and abide by necessity. Then you'll be close.

"It is easy to obliterate tracks, hard not to walk on the ground. It is easy to use falsehood in working for people; it is hard to use falsehood in working for nature.

"I have heard of flying with wings; I have never heard of flying without wings. I have heard of knowing with knowledge; I have never heard of knowing without knowledge.

"For those who gaze into space, the empty room produces white light; auspicious signs hover in stillness. But if one does not stay here, that is called galloping even while sitting.

"If you have your ears and eyes penetrate inwardly, and are detached from conceptual knowledge, then even if ghosts and spirits come after you they will stop; how much the more will people!"

Hui-tzu said to Chuang-tzu, "I have a gigantic tree, but its trunk is too gnarled for the plumb line and its branches too twisted for the ruler: even if it were set in the middle of the road, carpenters would pay no attention to it. What you say is similarly grandiose but useless, rejected by everyone alike."

Chuang-tzu replied, "Have you not seen a wild-cat? It lowers itself close to the ground to watch for careless prey; it leaps this way and that, light and low, but then gets caught in a trap and dies. A yak, on the other hand, is enormous; it can do big things, but cannot catch a rat. Now you have a huge tree and worry that it is useless: why not plant it in the vast plain of the homeland of Nothing Whatsoever, roaming in effortlessness by its side and sleeping in freedom beneath it? The reason it does not fall to the axe, and no one injures it, is that it cannot be exploited. So what's the trouble?"

HUAI-NAN-TZU

Heaven is calm and clear, earth is stable and peaceful. Beings who lose these qualities die, while those who emulate them live.

Calm spaciousness is the house of spiritual light; open selflessness is the abode of the Way.

Therefore there are those who seek it outwardly and lose it inwardly, and there are those who safeguard it inwardly and gain it outwardly.

The Way of heaven and earth is enormously vast, yet it still moderates its manifestation of glory and is sparing of its spiritual light. How then could human eyes and ears work perpetually, without rest? How could the vital spirit be forever rushing around without becoming exhausted?

Don't be surprised, don't be startled; all things will arrange themselves. Don't cause a disturbance, don't exert pressure; all things will clarify themselves.

Human nature is developed by profound serenity and lightness, virtue is developed by harmonious joy and open selflessness. When externals do not confuse you inwardly, your nature finds the condition that suits it; when your nature does not disturb harmony, virtue rests in its place.

If you can get through life in the world by developing your nature and embrace virtue to the end of your years, it can be said that you are able to embody the Tao.

If so, there will be no thrombosis or stagnation in your blood vessels, no depressing stifling energy in your organs. Calamity and fortune will not be able to disturb you, censure and praise will not be able to affect you. Therefore you can reach the ultimate.

When the mind neither sorrows nor delights, that is supreme attainment of virtue. To succeed without changing is supreme attainment of calm. To be unburdened by habitual desires is supreme attainment of emptiness. To have no likes and dislikes is supreme attainment of equanimity. Not getting mixed up with things is supreme attainment of purity.

Those who can accomplish these five things reach spiritual illumination. Those who reach spiritual illumination are those who attain the inward.

Therefore when you master the outward by means of the inward, all affairs are unspoiled.

If you can attain this within, then you can develop it outwardly.

When you attain it within, your internal organs are peaceful and your thoughts are calm; your muscles are strong, your eyes and ears are alert and clear. You have accurate perceptions and understanding; you are firm and strong without snapping.

In a small domain you are not cramped, in a large domain you are not careless. Your soul is not excited, your spirit is not disturbed. Serene and aloof, you are the toughest in the world. Sensitive and responsive, when pressed you can move, infinitely calm and inscrutable.

Human nature is generally such that it likes tranquillity and dislikes anxiety; it likes leisure and dislikes toil. When the mind is always desireless, this can be called tranquillity; when the body is always unoccupied, this can be called leisure.

If you set your mind free in tranquillity and relinquish your body in leisure, thereby to await the direction of nature, spontaneously happy within and free from hurry without, even the magnitude of the universe cannot change you at all; even should the sun and moon be eclipsed, that does not dampen your will. Then you are as if noble even if lowly, and you are as if rich even if poor.

When the spirit controls the body, the body obeys;

when the body overrules the spirit, the spirit is exhausted. Although intelligence is useful, it needs to be returned to the spirit. This is called the great harmony.

The mind is the ruler of the body, while the spirit is the treasure of the mind. When the body is worked without rest, it collapses. When the spirit is used without cease, it becomes exhausted. Sages value and respect them, and do not dare to be excessive.

Sages respond to being by nonbeing, unfailingly finding out the inner pattern; they receive fullness by emptiness, unfailingly finding out the measure. They live out their lives with calm joy and empty tranquillity. Therefore they are not too distant from anything and not too close to anything.

What sages learn is to return their nature to the beginning and let the mind travel freely in openness. What developed people learn is to link their nature to vast emptiness and become aware of the silent infinite.

The learning of ordinary worldlings is otherwise. They grasp at virtues and constrict their nature, inwardly worrying about their physical organs while outwardly belaboring their eyes and ears.

Sages send the spirit to the storehouse of awareness and return to the beginning of myriad things. They look at the formless, listen to the soundless. In the midst of profound darkness, they alone see light; in the midst of silent vastness, they alone have illumination.

When the perceptions are clear, with profound discernment free from seductive longings, and energy and will are open and calm, serenely joyful and free from habitual desires, then the internal organs are settled, full of energy that does not leak out. The vital spirit preserves the physical body inwardly and does not go outside. Then it is not difficult to see the precedents of the past and the aftermath of the future.

Outwardly go along with the flow, while inwardly keeping your true nature. Then your eyes and ears will not be dazzled, your thoughts will not be confused, while the spirit within you will expand greatly to roam in the realm of absolute purity.

When the spiritual light is stored in formlessness, vitality and energy return to perfect reality. Then the eyes are clear, but not used for looking; the ears are sharp, but not used for listening. The mind is expanded, but not used for thinking.

When vitality passes into the eyes, the vision is clear; when it is in the ears, the hearing is sharp. When it is in the mouth, speech is accurate; and when it gathers in the mind, thought is penetrating.

The energy of heaven is the higher soul, the energy of earth is the lower soul. Return them to the mystic chamber, so each is in its place. Keep watch over them and do not lose them; you will be connected to absolute unity above, and the vitality of absolute unity is connected to heaven.

There are countless sights, sounds, and flavors, rarities from distant lands, oddities and curiosities, that can change the aim of the mind, destabilize the vital spirit, and disturb the circulation and energy.

The vital spirit belongs to heaven, the physical body belongs to earth: when the vital spirit goes home and the physical body returns to its origin, where then is the self?

WEN-TZU

Lao-tzu said:

Consider the world light, and the spirit is not burdened; consider myriad things slight, and the mind is not confused. Consider life and death equal, and the intellect is not afraid; consider change as sameness, and clarity is not obscured.

Perfected people lean on a pillar that is never shaken, travel a road that is never blocked, are endowed from a resource that is never exhausted, and learn from a teacher that never dies. They are successful in whatever they undertake and arrive wherever they go. Whatever they do, they embrace destiny and go along without confusion. Calamity, fortune, profit, and harm cannot trouble their minds.

Those who act justly can be pressed by humanitarianism but cannot be threatened by arms; they can be corrected by righteousness but cannot be hooked by profit. Ideal people will die for justice and cannot be stayed by riches and rank.

Those who act justly cannot be intimidated by death; even less can those who do not act at all. Those who do not act deliberately have no burdens. Unburdened people use the world as the marker of a sundial: above they observe the ways of perfected people to delve deeply into the meanings of the Way and virtue; below they consider the behaviors customary in the world, which are enough to induce a feeling of shame.

Not doing anything with the world is the drum announcing learning.

Lao-tzu said:

Those who are known as Real People are united in essence with the Way, so they have endowments yet appear to have none; they are full yet appear to be empty. They govern the inside, not the outside. Clear and pure, utterly plain, they do not contrive artificialities but return to simplicity.

Comprehending the fundamental, embracing the spirit, thereby they roam the root of heaven and earth, wander beyond the dust and dirt, and travel to work at noninvolvement. Mechanical intelligence does not burden their minds; they watch what is not temporal and are not moved by things.

Seeing the evolution of events, they keep to the source. Their attention is focused internally, and they understand calamity and fortune in the context of unity. They sit unconscious of doing anything, they walk unconscious of going anywhere.

They know without learning, see without looking, succeed without striving, discern without comparing. They respond to feeling, act when pressed, and go when there is no choice, like the shining of light, like the casting of shadows. They take the Way as their guide; when there is any opposition they remain empty and open, clear and calm, and then the opposition disappears.

They consider a thousand lives as one evolution, they regard ten thousand differences as of one source. They have vitality but do not exploit it; they have spirit but do not make it labor. They keep to the simplicity of wholeness and stand in the center of the quintessential.

Lao-tzu said:

Those whom we call sages rest peacefully in their places according to the time and enjoy their work as appropriate to the age.

Sadness and happiness are deviations of virtue; likes and dislikes are a burden to the mind; joy and anger are excesses on the Way.

Therefore their birth is the action of nature, their death is the transformation of things.

When still, you merge with the quality of darkness; when active, you are on the same wave as light.

So mind is the master of form, spirit is the jewel

of mind. When the body is worked without rest, it collapses; when vitality is used without rest, it is exhausted. Therefore sages, heedful of this, do not dare to be excessive.

They use nonbeing to respond to being, and are sure to find out the reason; they use emptiness to receive fullness, and are sure to find out the measure. They pass their lives in peaceful serenity and open calm, neither alienating anyone nor cleaving to anyone.

Embracing virtue, they are warm and harmonious, thereby following Nature, meeting with the Way, and being near Virtue. They do not start anything for profit or initiate anything that would cause harm. Death and life cause no changes in the self, so it is called most spiritual. With the spirit, anything that is sought can be found, and anything that is done can be accomplished.

Lao-tzu said:

Rank, power, and wealth are things people crave, but when compared to the body they are insignificant. Therefore sages eat enough to fill emptiness and maintain energy, and dress sufficiently to cover their bodies and keep out the cold. They adjust to their real conditions and refuse the rest, not craving gain and not accumulating much.

Clarifying their eyes, they do not look; quieting their ears, they do not listen. Closing their mouths, they do not speak; letting their minds be, they do not think. Abandoning intellectualism, they return to utter simplicity; resting their vital spirit, they detach from knowledge. Therefore they have no likes or dislikes. This is called great attainment.

To get rid of pollution and eliminate burdens, nothing compares to never leaving the source. Then what action will not succeed?

Those who know how to nurture the harmony of life cannot be hooked by profit. Those who know how to join inside and outside cannot be seduced by power.

Beyond where there is no beyond is most great; within where there is no within is most precious. If you know the great and precious, where can you go and not succeed?

Lao-tzu said:

Those who practiced the Way in ancient times ordered their feelings and nature and governed their mental functions, nurturing them with harmony and keeping them in proportion. Enjoying the Way, they forgot about lowliness; secure in virtue, they forgot about poverty.

There was that which by nature they did not want, and since they had no desire for it they did not get it.

There was that which their hearts did not enjoy, and since they did not enjoy it they did not do it.

Whatever had no benefit to essential nature they did not allow to drag their virtue down; whatever had no advantage for life they did not allow to disturb harmony. They did not let themselves act or think arbitrarily, so their measures could be regarded as models for the whole world.

They ate according to the size of their bellies, dressed to fit their bodies, lived in enough room to accommodate them, acted in accord with their true condition.

They considered the world extra and did not try to possess it; they left everyone and everything to themselves and did not seek profit. How could they lose their essential life because of poverty or riches, high or low social status?

Those who are like this can be called able to understand and embody the Way.

Lao-tzu said:

The energy that people receive from nature is one in terms of the feelings of the senses toward sound, form, scent, and temperature. But the way in which it is managed differs: some die thereby, and some live thereby; some become exemplary people, some become petty people.

The spirit is where knowledge gathers; when the

spirit is clear, knowledge is illumined. Knowledge is the seat of the heart; when knowledge is objective, the heart is even.

The reason people use limpid water for a mirror, not a moving stream, is that it is clear and still. Thus when the spirit is clear and the attention is even, it is then possible to discern people's true conditions.

Therefore use of this inevitably depends on not exploiting. When a mirror is clear, dust does not dirty it; when the spirit is clear, habitual cravings do not delude it.

So if the mind goes anywhere, the spirit is there in a state of arousal; if you return it to emptiness, that will extinguish compulsive activity, so it can be at rest. This is the freedom of sages. This is why those who govern the world must realize the true condition of essence and life before they can do so.

Lao-tzu said:

Sages close up together with darkness and open up together with light. Able to reach the point where there is no enjoyment, they find there is nothing they do not enjoy. Since there is nothing they do not enjoy, they reach the pinnacle of enjoyment.

They use the inner to make the external enjoyable, and do not use externals to make the inner enjoyable; therefore they have spontaneous enjoyment in themselves, and so have their own will, which is esteemed by the world. The reason it is so is that this is essential to the world in the world's own terms.

It is not up to another, but up to oneself; it is not up to anyone but the individual. When the individual attains it, everything is included.

So those who understand the logic of mental functions regard desires, cravings, likes, and dislikes as externals. Therefore nothing delights them, nothing angers them, nothing pleases them, nothing pains them. Everything is mysteriously the same; nothing is wrong, nothing is right.

So there is consistent logic for men and consistent behavior for women: they do not need authority to be noble, they do not need riches to be wealthy, they do not need strength to be powerful; they do not exploit material goods, do not crave social reputation, do not consider high social status to be safe and do not consider low social status to be dangerous; their body, spirit, energy, and will each abides in its proper place.

The body is the house of life; energy is the basis of life; spirit is the controller of life: if one loses its position, all three are injured. Therefore when the spirit is in the lead, the body follows it, with beneficial results; when the body is in the lead, the spirit follows it, with harmful results. Those people whose lives are gluttony and lust are tripped and blinded by power and profit, seduced and charmed by fame and status, nearly beyond human conception.

When your rank is high in the world, then your vitality and spirit are depleted daily, eventually to become dissipated and not return to the body. If you close up inside and keep them out, they have no way to enter. For this reason there are sometimes problems with absentmindedness and work being forgotten.

When the vitality, spirit, will, and energy are calm, they fill you day by day and make you strong. When they are hyperactive, they are depleted day by day, making you old.

Therefore sages keep nurturing their spirit, make their energy gentle, make their bodies normal, and bob with the Way. In this way they keep company with the evolution of all things and respond to the changes in all events.

Their sleep is dreamless, their knowledge is traceless, their action is formless, their stillness is bodiless. When they are present, it is as if they were absent; they are alive, but are as if dead. They can appear and disappear instantaneously, and can employ ghosts and spirits.

The capabilities of vitality and spirit elevate them to the Way, causing vitality and spirit to expand to their fullest effectiveness without losing the source.

Day and night, without a gap, they are like spring to living beings. This is harmonizing and producing the seasons in the heart.

So the physical body may pass away, but the spirit does not change. Use the unchanging to respond to changes, and there is never any limit. What changes returns to formlessness, while what does not change lives together with the universe.

So what gives birth to life is not itself born; what it gives birth to is what is born. What produces change does not itself change; what it changes is what changes. This is where real people roam, the path of quintessence.

Tales of Inner Meaning

INTRODUCTION

Fables, stories, and jokes have been used by practical philosophers for thousands of years as a means of conveying ideas and impressions to the receptive mind. They are particularly useful for subtleties that do not translate well into formal logic, and for making a direct impression, bypassing intellectual prejudices in the mind of the reader. Several examples of such tales of inner meaning are presented in this section of the present anthology.

The first group of stories is drawn from the Lieh-tzu (*Lie zi*), a well-known classic and source of numerous popular tales whose currency has long since expanded beyond the realm of Taoism per se. There is a wide range of opinion about the date of this text, a question to which there would appear to be no satisfactory solution in conventional historical terms. For the purposes of the present translations, the extent of the significance of this matter is that there appear to be additions and comments that flatten some of the tales and tend to diffuse rather than clarify their inner Taoist meaning. Therefore the stories from Lieh-tzu are rendered here in forms reflecting a synthesis of the written text and oral tradition.

The Learned Man

One day Confucius was walking along with some disciples when they came upon two boys arguing. Confucius asked the boys what the dispute was about. They told him they were arguing about whether the sun was nearer at dawn and farther away at noon, or farther away at dawn and nearer at noon.

One of the boys argued that the sun appeared larger at dawn and smaller at noon, so it must be closer at dawn and farther away at noon.

The other boy argued that it was cool at dawn and hot at noon, so the sun must be farther away at dawn and closer at noon.

Confucius was at a loss to determine which one was correct. The boys jeered at him, "Who said you were so smart?"

The Story of Old Mister Shang

Old Mister Shang was a poor peasant whose strange fate began to unfold on the day his ramshackle little house was commandeered by a couple of arrogant young men belonging to the establishment of a local gangster.

At that time wealthy families, with many followers and hangers-on, could be as if a law unto themselves. Some families might have thousands of armed men on their estates. The gangster in question was the head of one such clan, and his followers were all young bullies from local well-to-do families. They spent their time dressing up in costly attire and gallivanting around, doing as they pleased.

The boss of the clan was well known for being able to make a poor man rich or a rich man poor with a single word or a nod of the head. Even the government had him on the payroll, though he had no regard whatsoever for law and order and contributed nothing at all to the general well-being. Countless were the deluded young men who had been maimed or killed in senseless duels staged to fire the ambitions of yet other deluded young men, and to amuse the gangster and his gang.

Old Mister Shang thought he had discovered his chance to become a success when he overheard the two young men that had taken over his house talking about their leader. The very next day old Shang set out for the residence of the gangster, who was such a big man that even the government paid him not to secede from the empire.

When old Shang arrived, he was greeted with hoots and hollers of laughter and derision. Who was this bumpkin, come to join their gang? Clearly he was going to be no fun for a duel, so the boys decided to see how it looked when an old man hit the ground after a fall from a building seven stories high.

A number of young men took poor old Shang up this high tower and told him the boss was offering a hundred pieces of gold to anyone who would jump off. Several of them made for the railing, as if to be the ones to get the prize, so old Shang hurriedly jumped over.

The hooligans held their breaths for a moment as they prepared to see the old man plummet to a gruesome death. What met their eyes instead was the sight of old Shang drifting lightly to the earth like a feather in the air.

Unable to believe what they had seen, the young

men dismissed it as a fluke, due perhaps to the sudden gust of wind that everyone had noticed.

Next they decided to take him to the river bend, where there was an infamous rapids full of holes with unmeasured depths. They told him of an enormous pearl lying at the bottom of a deep hole under the swift current, and said the boss had offered it to anyone who could fish it out.

Old Shang plunged into the current without a moment's hesitation, only to surface moments later holding a huge pearl in his hand.

This could no longer be passed off as a fluke, and old Shang was now given a place among the guests of the master of the house.

Not long after that, a fire broke out in the storehouse. The boss told his followers that he would reward anyone who could retrieve his silk. Old Shang rushed right into the burning building and emerged unscorched with the silk.

At this point, the hooligans were convinced that old Shang must be one of those who had attained the Tao, and they all begged forgiveness for having tricked him. They said, "We played tricks on you, not realizing you were one of those imbued with the Tao. We derided you, unaware you were a man of the spirit. You must think us ignorant, deaf, and blind indeed, but we wish to ask about your Way."

Old Shang said, "You mean you were joking?"

When this was reported to Confucius, he said, "Someone who is perfectly sincere can affect things thereby. Old Shang believed in falsehoods, and things did not betray his trust. How much the more effective would truth and sincerity on both sides be. Make a note of this."

The Poor Man and the Gold

A poor man decided one day to get rich, so he put on his hat and coat and went to town.

As he walked through the center of town, pondering the question of how to obtain riches, his glance happened to fall on someone carrying a quantity of gold.

The poor man rushed up and grabbed some of the gold. He was caught as he tried to flee.

The magistrate asked the poor man, "How did you expect to get away with the gold, with all those people around?"

"I only saw the gold," explained the poor man, "I didn't see the people."

Who for Whom

Once a man held a huge banquet with a thousand guests. When someone presented a gift of fish and fowl, the host said appreciatively, "Heaven is generous to the people indeed, planting cereals and creating fish and fowl for our use." The huge crowd of guests echoed this sentiment.

A youth about twelve years old, however, who had been sitting in the most remote corner of the banquet hall, now came forward and said to the host, "It is not as you say, sir. All beings in the universe are living creatures on a par with us. No species is higher or lower in rank than another, it's just that they control each other by differences in their intelligence and power; they eat each other, but that does not mean they were produced for each other. People take what they can eat and eat it, but does that mean that heaven produced that for people? If so, then since mosquitoes bite skin and tigers and wolves eat flesh, does that not mean that heaven made humans for the mosquitoes and created flesh for tigers and wolves?"

Suspicion

Once a man found that his axe was missing, and suspected his neighbor's son of having taken it. Observing the youth walking around, the man was convinced that his was the walk of a thief. The youth looked like a thief and talked like a thief; everything he did pointed to his having stolen the axe.

Then one day the man happened to find his missing axe. After that, he noticed his neighbor's son wasn't behaving like a thief anymore.

Ups and Downs

Mr. Yin of the state of Chou was a prosperous businessman. His employees worked without rest from early morning until late at night.

Among them was an old laborer whose physical strength was virtually exhausted, yet who worked all the harder for that. By day he did his work huffing and puffing, grunting and groaning; by night he slept soundly, thoroughly exhausted.

As the old worker slept, his spirit relaxed and expanded. Every night he dreamed he was a king, a leader of the people, commanding the affairs of the nation, roaming at leisure and reveling in villas, enjoying whatever he wanted, his delight beyond compare. When he woke up, he would go back to work.

When someone expressed pity at how hard the old man toiled, he responded, "People may live a hundred years, but that is divided half and half into day and night. In the daytime I work like a slave, and I can't deny that it is miserable. At night, however, I am a king, and my pleasure is incomparable. So what have I got to complain about?"

As for the boss, Mr. Yin, his mind was occupied with his business, his thoughts concentrated on his affairs, so his body and mind were both tired. At night he also collapsed with fatigue into a deep sleep. Every night he dreamed he was a servant, rushing around all the time doing one chore after another, being scolded and beaten time and again. So he used to huff and puff and grunt and groan the whole night through.

Mr. Yin was unhappy about this state of affairs and consulted a friend about it. His friend said, "You have status and wealth far beyond that of most people, but at night you say you dream you are a servant. Well, the alternation of suffering and ease is normal; if you want to have it good both in working life and dream life, I'm afraid that is asking too much."

After that Mr. Yin lightened his workers' load and reduced his own concerns, so both got a bit of relief.

Forgetfulness

A man named Hua-tzu suffered from forgetfulness when he reached middle age. He would forget by nighttime what he had gotten during the day, and he would forget by morning what he had given at night. On the road he would forget to walk, at home he would forget to sit down. At any given time he was unconscious of what had gone before, and later he would not know what was going on at the present.

His whole family was distressed by his condition. They called on a fortune-teller to figure it out, but there was no prognosis. They called on a shaman to pray for him, but that did not stop it. They called on a doctor to treat him, but that did not cure it.

Now there was a Confucian who reckoned he could heal the man, and his wife and children offered him half of their estate for the remedy. The Confucian said, "This cannot be figured out by omens, cannot be alleviated by prayer, cannot be treated by medicine. I will try to transform his mind and change his thought, in hopes that he will get better."

Now when the Confucian tested him by exposing him to the elements, the man asked for clothing. When he starved him, the man asked for food. When he shut him up in the dark, the man asked for light. The Confucian joyfully announced to the children, "This sickness can be cured. My remedy, however, is secret and not to be revealed to others. Please clear everyone out and leave me alone with him for seven days." The family did as he said, so no one knew what measures the Confucian took, but one day the ailment from which the man had suffered for years was all gone.

When the man woke up, he flew into a rage. He threw his wife out of the house, punished his children, and went after the Confucian with a hatchet. The local people grabbed him and asked him what it was all about. He said, "In my past forgetfulness I was clear and free, unaware even of the existence or nonexistence of heaven and earth. Now that I am suddenly conscious, all these decades of gains and losses, sorrows and joys, likes and dislikes, suddenly occur to me in a welter of confusion. I am afraid that future gains and losses, sorrows and joys, likes and dislikes, will disturb my mind like this. Will I ever have a moment's forgetfulness again?"

The Ailment

Lung Shu said to the physician Wen Chi, "Your art is subtle. I have an ailment; can you cure it?"

The physician said, "I will do as you say, but first tell me about your symptoms."

Lung Shu said, "I am not honored when the whole village praises me, nor am I ashamed when the whole county criticizes me. Gain does not make me happy, loss does not grieve me. I look upon life as like death, and see wealth as like poverty. I view people as like pigs, and see myself as like others. At home I am as though at an inn, and I look upon my native village as like a foreign country. With these afflictions, rewards cannot encourage me, punishments cannot threaten me. I cannot be changed by flourishing or decline, gain or loss; I cannot be moved by sorrow or happiness. Thus I cannot serve the government, associate with friends, run my household, or control my servants. What sickness is this? Is there any way to cure it?"

The physician had Lung Shu stand with his back to the light while he looked into his chest. After a while he said, "Aha! I see your heart; it is empty! You are nearly a sage. Six of the apertures in your heart are open, one of them is closed. This may be why you think the wisdom of a sage is an ailment. It cannot be stopped by my shallow art."

Golden Butterflies

In the time of the emperor Mu-tsung (Muzong) of the T'ang dynasty, in the ninth century, among the members of the elite corps of the imperial guard was a Japanese man named Kan Shiwa.

Kan Shiwa was a most extraordinary sculptor. He could fashion any sort of bird and make it so that it could drink water, hop around, stretch out its neck and call, and so on, all in the most beautiful and charming manner. He put machinery in the bellies of the birds he made, so that besides having beautiful plumage they could also fly one or two hundred feet in the air.

Also, Shiwa sculpted cats that could do even more; they could run around and even catch small birds.

Now the captain of the guard thought this was truly marvelous, and wrote to the emperor about it. Emperor Mu-tsung summoned Kan Shiwa into his presence, and he too was captivated by Shiwa's skill.

The emperor asked Shiwa if he could carve something yet more marvelous. Shiwa told the emperor he would make a "dais for seeing dragons."

The Story of Wan Baochang

Wan Baochang (Pao-ch'ang) was a man of unknown origin. A born genius, he had a subtle understanding of music and crafted all sorts of musical instruments.

Once when he was in the wilds, he saw a group of ten people dressed in beautiful clothes riding on magnificent bannered chariots. They were standing in rows, as if waiting on someone.

Wan moved to get out of their way, but they sent someone to summon him to them. When he approached, they said to him, "You have been given a musical nature, and you are going to hand on eight kinds of musical instruments in a degenerate age, to save its music from imminent corruption. But you do not yet completely know all the sounds of correct beginnings, so the supreme God has sent officers of the highest heaven to show you the mysterious and subtle essentials."

Then they had Wan sit there while they taught him the music of the ages, the sounds of order and disturbance. They set forth everything in detail, and Wan recorded it all. After a while, the group of immortals took off into the sky, and Wan went back home. When he returned, he found that he had been gone for five days. After this he studied all the music of the human world.

During the Northern Zhou and Sui dynasties in the latter sixth century, Wan gained recognition for his unusual talent and learning. He did not serve in government, however, and lived a bohemian life-style.

In the early 590s, when a certain nobleman completed a musical composition and submitted it to the throne for official adoption as court music for the newly established Sui dynasty, Emperor Wen summoned Wan to consult him. After listening to it, Wan said, "This is the sound of the destruction of a nation: sad, bitter, fleeting, scattered. It is not the sound of true elegance. It will not do for classical music."

The emperor had Wan make musical instruments. All of the instruments he made were low-keyed, different from those in use hitherto. Wan also said there was a mode in the ritual music of the ancient Chou dynasty nearly two thousand years earlier that none of the experts had been able to understand for centuries. When he composed a piece in this mode, people all laughed in derision, but when he had it performed, everyone marveled.

Subsequently Wan readjusted countless instruments, but their resulting tone wa and serene, not in accord with popular they never became fashionable.

When Wan heard a musical compositic "Forever and Ever," he wept and told peop licentious, harsh, and sad; it won't be lon people are killing each other everywhere."

Now at this time there was peace throug land and the economy was flourishing, so e who heard this statement of Wan's thought all wrong. But by the end of the era of Grea [618, when the Sui dynasty collapsed], Wan proved to be true.

Wan Baochang had no children and wa doned by his wife. He passed away in lonelin sorrow, intimating that he had been punis heaven for becoming too passionately involve the world.

The Story of Wan Baochang

Wan Baochang (Pao-ch'ang) was a man of unknown origin. A born genius, he had a subtle understanding of music and crafted all sorts of musical instruments.

Once when he was in the wilds, he saw a group of ten people dressed in beautiful clothes riding on magnificent bannered chariots. They were standing in rows, as if waiting on someone.

Wan moved to get out of their way, but they sent someone to summon him to them. When he approached, they said to him, "You have been given a musical nature, and you are going to hand on eight kinds of musical instruments in a degenerate age, to save its music from imminent corruption. But you do not yet completely know all the sounds of correct beginnings, so the supreme God has sent officers of the highest heaven to show you the mysterious and subtle essentials."

Then they had Wan sit there while they taught him the music of the ages, the sounds of order and disturbance. They set forth everything in detail, and Wan recorded it all. After a while, the group of immortals took off into the sky, and Wan went back home. When he returned, he found that he had been gone for five days. After this he studied all the music of the human world.

During the Northern Zhou and Sui dynasties in the latter sixth century, Wan gained recognition for his unusual talent and learning. He did not serve in government, however, and lived a bohemian lifestyle.

In the early 590s, when a certain nobleman completed a musical composition and submitted it to the throne for official adoption as court music for the newly established Sui dynasty, Emperor Wen summoned Wan to consult him. After listening to it, Wan said, "This is the sound of the destruction of a nation: sad, bitter, fleeting, scattered. It is not the sound of true elegance. It will not do for classical music."

The emperor had Wan make musical instruments. All of the instruments he made were low-keyed, different from those in use hitherto. Wan also said there was a mode in the ritual music of the ancient Chou dynasty nearly two thousand years earlier that none of the experts had been able to understand for centuries. When he composed a piece in this mode, people all laughed in derision, but when he had it performed, everyone marveled.

Subsequently Wan readjusted countless musical instruments, but their resulting tone was elegant and serene, not in accord with popular tastes; so they never became fashionable.

When Wan heard a musical composition called "Forever and Ever," he wept and told people, "It is licentious, harsh, and sad; it won't be long before people are killing each other everywhere."

Now at this time there was peace throughout the land and the economy was flourishing, so everyone who heard this statement of Wan's thought he was all wrong. But by the end of the era of Great Works [618, when the Sui dynasty collapsed], Wan's words proved to be true.

Wan Baochang had no children and was abandoned by his wife. He passed away in loneliness and sorrow, intimating that he had been punished by heaven for becoming too passionately involved with the world.

Golden Butterflies

In the time of the emperor Mu-tsung (Muzong) of the T'ang dynasty, in the ninth century, among the members of the elite corps of the imperial guard was a Japanese man named Kan Shiwa.

Kan Shiwa was a most extraordinary sculptor. He could fashion any sort of bird and make it so that it could drink water, hop around, stretch out its neck and call, and so on, all in the most beautiful and charming manner. He put machinery in the bellies of the birds he made, so that besides having beautiful plumage they could also fly one or two hundred feet in the air.

Also, Shiwa sculpted cats that could do even more; they could run around and even catch small birds.

Now the captain of the guard thought this was truly marvelous, and wrote to the emperor about it. Emperor Mu-tsung summoned Kan Shiwa into his presence, and he too was captivated by Shiwa's skill.

The emperor asked Shiwa if he could carve something yet more marvelous. Shiwa told the emperor he would make a "dais for seeing dragons."

Several days later, the dais was done. It was two feet high and looked like an ordinary footstool. When he saw it, the emperor wondered what was so special about it. Shiwa told him he would soon see if he stepped up onto the dais.

Not without misgivings, the emperor stepped up. The moment he did so, a gigantic dragon appeared in the sky. It was about twice the size of a man and had scales, a mane, claws, and horns; it flew into the clouds and rode on a mist, dancing in the sky. Its energy and appearance were such that one would never think it to have been made by human hands.

The emperor was flabbergasted. Frantically he jumped off the little platform and said, "Fine, fine, very good—now take it away with you!"

Strange to say, the moment he got off the dais the big dragon disappeared. All that remained was to put it back in its place.

Now Shiwa apologized to the emperor for startling him so, and offered to make good by doing something amusing.

The emperor, after protesting that he had not been frightened but merely surprised, asked Shiwa what he intended to fashion.

"Something small," replied Shiwa, producing a box from his pocket. When he opened it up, inside were little scarlet bugs.

"What are they?" the emperor asked.

"They're like spiders," said Shiwa. "They're fly-catchers."

"Are they real?" the emperor asked, amazed by their lifelike quality.

"No, they're manmade," Shiwa answered.

"Then why are they scarlet?" asked the emperor.

"Because I feed them cinnabar powder," Shiwa explained. "Similarly," he continued, "if I fed them sulfur they'd be golden, and if I fed them powdered pearl they'd be pearly."

Then the emperor asked what the insects could do. Shiwa said, "They will dance for Your Majesty. And so that we may have Your Majesty view the dance, I have invited the musicians to play 'The Song of Liang-chou,' which is the insects' favorite tune." Now as the musicians prepared to play, the little red spiders scrambled out of the box and arranged themselves in five rows. They now stood in formation, waiting for the music to start.

When the orchestra began to play, the spiders began a very orderly dance in harmony with the music. They went forward, then backward; the rows came together, then rearrayed at angles, now suddenly shifted to form a circle.

The choreography was beautiful indeed, resembling an intricate and picturesque brocade, truly dazzling to the eye. And as the music played, the spiders also made a humming sound, as loud as the buzzing of a fly, keeping time with the music.

Finally, when the music ended, the spiders went back to their beginning position, arrayed in five rows; in unison they bowed to the emperor, and then went in orderly files back into the box.

The emperor exclaimed his delight. Shiwa went on to explain that the spiders were, as their name suggested, indeed flycatching bugs. To demonstrate, he took one of them and placed it on the palm of his hand; pointing to a fly near a tree, he said, "Grab it." The spider caught the fly just as a hawk might catch a sparrow. Then spiders leaped from Shiwa's hand to catch flies alighting on people's shoulders, or even flies buzzing through the air. Catching the flies, one by one they returned to Shiwa's palm.

The emperor marveled at this. He gave Shiwa a big reward of silver, which Shiwa ungrudgingly gave away to poor people in the city. Now the rumor passed around among the people of the city was that Kan Shiwa was a spiritual immortal from the Isles of the Blest in the Eastern Sea. Just when this gossip reached its peak, Kan Shiwa disappeared from the imperial guard, and no one ever saw him again.

Meanwhile, Emperor Mu-tsung had planted his garden with the finest and most luxuriant peonies, which filled the palace with their fragrance in season. Every evening, myriads of butterflies danced and chased each other amidst these blossoms.

Strange to say, the butterflies were all golden or pearly, and their dazzling brilliance made the palace seem as beautiful as the celestial realms. Countless thousands of them appeared in the evenings, but not one was to be found in the morning.

Every evening the palace ladies would vie with one another to catch these beautiful butterflies, and they found it very easy to do so. They used silk thread to tie the butterflies to their bosoms, or to their hairpins.

These shining butterflies, used as ornaments, were very pretty indeed, but when morning came, they were found to have lost their sheen, so the girls took them off. Then the following evening the butterflies would come to life again, flashing their brilliant lights as they danced among the flowers.

At these times Emperor Mu-tsung would roam around the garden happily, but what he liked most was to catch several hundred of the butterflies, let them loose in the palace, and enjoy watching the palace girls chase them.

The emperor enjoyed this sport every evening, never tiring of it, until one day the butterflies did not return to the flower garden. Emperor Mu-tsung and his ladies thought they had caught them all, but that wasn't so. Wherever flowers grew throughout the city, there now began to appear these strange and beautiful butterflies. They proved to be especially easy to catch among the flowers and trees planted by poor people; and so the poor would often catch them and sell them to rich people for a high price, using the proceeds to purchase things they needed.

One day the emperor went to his treasure house to get a certain dish made of gold. When he got there, he found that his precious article had already been smashed to pieces, and so had other items of gold and pearl.

From the midst of the fragments he could vaguely discern the pattern of a butterfly, and at that moment realized that the missing butterflies were the work of Kan Shiwa. He immediately searched the whole treasure house, but could find no trace of the wizard. After that he had the palace and the whole capital city, from its avenues to its alleyways, searched thoroughly, but the man was never found again.

And the butterflies never returned.

The Story of Nieh Shih-tao

Nieh Shih-tao was styled One Who Had Penetrated the Subtle. He was a brilliant man, yet simple and straightforward. Modest and prudent in his speech and behavior, he was known for taking care of his parents well in their old age, and was highly respected in his community. When he was young, he became the student of one of those beyond convention. At the age of thirteen, he was ordained as a Taoist priest, and at the age of fifteen received an esoteric symbol of a method for cultivating reality.

According to his own account, once when he was reading Taoist books he came across a prescription for eating pine sap and decided to climb Hundred Fathoms Mountain with a Taoist colleague to gather some sap.

This mountain was very steep and high, and from its peak one had a view of all four directions. At night the two Taoists rested under the pines on the summit of the mountain; the sky was clear, the moon was bright. Suddenly they heard immortal music coming from Purple Cloud Mountain to the southeast, far far away, slowly passing Stone and Metal Mountain, which was the same height as Hundred Fathoms Mountain and, though ten miles away on the surface of the earth, seemed very close from peak to peak.

When they heard the immortal music reach them, it stopped a while; then there were three beats of a small drum, and a whole orchestra was clearly heard to play again. Though percussion instruments kept a beat, it was impossible to determine the melody. The sounds were high and clear, not like the music of the human world. It continued from midnight until dawn, finally stopping at cock crow.

Later they heard from the villagers who lived at the foot of the mountain that they had all heard it. Nieh's colleague said, "When we were gathering mystic medicine, we suddenly heard immortal music. This must mean that our intentions have been felt in the other world. I also regard it as a sign that you will attain the Tao."

After that, Nieh traveled around, then went to Nanyue, the southern Holy Mountain, where he prostrated himself before the altars of Jade Purity and Blue Jade of the Heaven of Light. Subsequently he stayed at the Immortal Summoning Observatory and entered the Wellspring of the Spirit of Open Clarity.

Now it was springtime, and he heard that the old

hermitage of Real Human Ts'ai (Cai), a famous adept of centuries past, was not far away. He also heard there were strange flowers and trees around there, and that woodcutters sometimes saw Real Human Ts'ai.

Nieh Shih-tao, delighted at the prospect of possibly getting to see Real Human Ts'ai, fasted for seven days to purify himself, then rose early one morning and went alone into the mountains.

As he went along, he smelled an unusual floral fragrance. Before he realized it, it was already evening, and he found himself by a large valley stream. He saw a woodcutter sitting on the sand, facing the water. Nieh quickened his steps, heading over toward the woodcutter, who now picked up his bundle and began to go down the valley.

The woodcutter turned around and looked at Nieh, then put his bundle back down and asked, "Where are you going, all alone?"

Nieh replied, "I'm doing my best to learn the Tao and find the immortals. I've heard Real Human Ts'ai is hidden in these mountains, and I just want to meet him once."

The woodcutter said, "Master Ts'ai's abode is extremely deep—people can't go there."

Nieh said, "I've already come this far, climbing

vines up cliffs—if there are mountains to cross, what does distance matter?"

The woodcutter said, "Anyway, it's getting late, almost nightfall; for now, go past this mountain, and to the east you'll find a home where you can stay."

Nieh wanted to go along with the woodcutter, but the woodcutter quickly stepped into the stream. It seemed quite shallow when the woodcutter walked in, but the moment Nieh stepped in, the stream turned out to be extremely deep, with a swift current. So Nieh did not dare try to wade across.

The woodcutter said, "You'll be able to cross this stream fifty years from now."

Nieh watched as the woodcutter walked across the water and disappeared out of sight on the farther shore.

Nieh then went several miles around the mountain and saw in the distance a rustic cottage with a fenced yard, chickens, and dogs. Approaching nearer, he saw a pale man who looked like a farmer, about thirty years old, living alone.

When this man saw Nieh, he thought it very odd that anyone would be traveling alone deep in the mountains. Suddenly he said, "The troubles of the family come out together; who is in charge?" And he asked Nieh, "Where are you going?"

Nieh said, "I'm looking for the hermitage of Real Human Ts'ai."

The man said, "Did you see a woodcutter on the way here?"

Nieh said that he had.

The man said, "That was the Taoist adept Ts'ai, who just passed by."

When Nieh heard this, he prostrated himself in prayer and said, "When an ordinary ignoramus meets an immortal sage and does not recognize him, that too is in the order of things."

It was already nightfall, and the mountain forest was pitch black. Nieh had no place to stay.

The man asked him, "Where do you come from?"

In reply, Nieh told him of his beginnings and his journey in search of reality. Then the man allowed him into the house and even had him sit on the platform near the fireplace.

The man said, "I happen to be out of provisions here in the mountains."

Nieh said, "I've been fasting a long time, and I'm not hungry." He saw beside the fire a kettle of hot water and several covered yellow porcelain bowls.

The host said, "You can drink what's in the bowls—feel free to take what you want."

Nieh then took the cover off one of the bowls

and found that there was tea in it. The host told him to pour hot water on it and drink.

Drinking the tea, Nieh found that its energy and savor were far different from ordinary tea. After a time he again wanted some tea and went to take the cover off another bowl, but found that he could not do so. He tried all the bowls, but found that he could not uncover any of them. Realizing with some diffidence that this was not an ordinary villager's house, he did not dare say anything.

The host, who slept in another room, did not get up the next morning even though the sun was high in the sky. And there was no fire in the hearth. In his sleep, the host said, "In this solitary and desolate place, suddenly I am concerned that I have nothing to offer you. There are a lot of homes in the village up ahead—you should go there."

Nieh went a couple of miles, but didn't see any houses, nothing but cliffs and defiles. When he turned around and looked back, he found that he had lost the way to where he had stayed the night. He went about ten miles, when he suddenly saw an old man.

Nieh and the old man sat on a flat rock to talk, and the old man asked him about why he had ventured into the mountains. Nieh told him all that had happened. The old man said, "Master Ts'ai and his son both hide in these mountains. Last night you stayed with his son."

The old man also told Nieh, "You have a rich air of the Tao about you, but your immortal bones are not yet complete. You will starve and thirst in the mountains—how can you stay here long?"

Then the old man suddenly broke off a stalk of a plant and handed it to Nieh. It was shaped like a ginger sprout and was over a foot long. Nieh chewed it and found it sweet and delicious. The old man also had him drink some spring water.

When Nieh raised his head after drinking from the spring, he found the old man had already disappeared.

Now Nieh was very disappointed, but after having taken the tea and eaten the herb, he felt stronger and lighter than when he had come.

He wanted to follow the mountain trail to look for a place to stay, but the trail was already covered and blocked by brambles and vines, impossible to get through.

So Nieh returned to the Immortal Summoning Observatory, where the Taoist priests there exclaimed with surprise, "This observatory is near the spiritual crags, but there are many poisonous creatures and wild beasts, so people are rarely able to go alone. We were wondering why you suddenly left over a month ago, and we've been worrying about you for a long time."

Nieh said, "I just left yesterday, and only stayed overnight."

He then told all about seeing the woodcutter, the cottage where he spent the night, and also about meeting the old man. The priests were impressed. They said, "While we have been living in this observatory, we have just been studying Taoism; we knew of the existence of Real Human Ts'ai, but haven't had any opportunities to see him. You must have the Tao in you already, because you've now seen both Master Ts'ai and his son. And as for the old man, in the past it has been said that Real Human P'eng also is hidden in these mountains; maybe the old man was this Master P'eng. As soon as you go into the mountains, you meet three immortals, and spend a day and a night there that is over a month long in the human world. In reality, this is what accumulated practice has led you to."

Nieh himself was amazed. He stayed at Immortal Summoning Observatory for years. Later he decided to return to his native place because his parents were getting old; he went back to the mountain hermitage near his home, where he had stayed as a youth.

When he went into the mountains to gather firewood and herbs, if he ran into tigers or leopards, when they saw Nieh they would let their ears droop and wag their tails, crouching down to the ground. Nieh would pet and talk to them, and they would get up and follow him. Sometimes he would fasten kindling or herbs on their backs; they would carry it home for him and then leave.

There are many similar examples of how people of the Way could influence wild animals. There was a mountain nearby where Nieh lived that was notorious for being inhabited by many fierce animals that didn't harm people; this was attributed to Nieh's influence.

His parents asked him how he had benefited from his traveling studies, and he told them the whole story. His parents were very happy because not only did they receive his care on the ordinary plane, they were also enriched by the all-embracing Tao through him. They considered themselves very fortunate to be the parents of Nieh.

Later he went traveling again, having heard that Real Human Mei and Administrator Siao were hiding on Jade Tube Mountain, and that many people of the time had seen them. Mei was Mei Fu, and had been an official; Siao was a prince of the Liang dynasty (sixth century C.E.), Siao Tzu-yun. When the governor of their district fled the rebellion of the infamous Hou Ching, whole families went into the mountains, and these two had both attained the Tao here.

Nieh, staying for a while at the Observatory of Pure Space on Jade Tube Mountain, wanted to look for Mei and Siao, so he made a special trip in hopes of seeing them. He set off with determination and went very deep into the mountains. Suddenly he saw a man dressed in muslin, with a black silk cap. By his face, he appeared to be about fifty years old.

Nieh paid his respects to this man and asked him who he was. At first the man said he was a worker and asked Nieh where he was going. Nieh told him he was looking for Mei and Siao. The worker said, "We have heard you are very diligent in your quest for the Tao, traveling to all the famous mountains. This is not easy at all. If you want to see those two masters, I can take you there. Your past deeds are very pure, already worthy of a name on the Jade Register; though you will not go on the ultimate flight right away, you will still cross over the world."

The workman also said, "I am Hsieh T'ung-hsiu (Xie Tongxiu). You may not know me, so I introduce myself. I have been living in seclusion in the mountains with the immortals P'eng and Ts'ai for three hundred years now. I know you have traveled to the Spring of Clear Awareness; I happen to have been ordered by the Master of the Eastern Flower to take charge of the mountain, forest, and earth immortals on Jade Tube Mountain, and am also in charge of the sanctuary shrines of the Observatory of Pure Space, so you and I have a spiritual connection already. That is why we have been able to meet. As for Master Mei and Master Siao, during the day they were called by the king of the Heaven of Little Existence, and I doubt that they will be back soon, so there is no use in waiting for them."

Nieh now bowed respectfully and said, "Mortals in the ordinary world search for the Tao in the wrong way, freezing their spirits and concentrating their thoughts from morning to night without yet knowing the essential wonder. They are like people adrift in a shoreless ocean. This unexpected meeting with you today is really a rare bit of good luck for me, as I have gotten to see a master of the Tao."

T'ung-hsiu said, "Your sincere devotion is very touching. You haven't finished your tasks in the world, so I am going to show you a way out of the mountains. We'll go to where I stay."

Nieh followed T'ung-hsiu for a couple of miles, when suddenly he saw a two-room reed house, very new and clean. Inside were low platform seats and a little kettle over a fire, with water boiling in it. It looked like a scholar's studio, with no one there.

T'ung-hsiu had Nieh come in and sit on a wooden horse, while T'ung-hsiu himself sat on a white stone deer. Suddenly a child came in and gave Nieh a cup of hot water. When he drank it, Nieh felt very clear and refreshed.

T'ung-hsiu also had him take a book from the shelf. He said, "This is the Basic Book. Be diligent in learning it, and you will attain the essence of reality."

Nieh wanted to stay there and learn from T'ung-hsiu, but before he said anything, T'ung-hsiu, aware of what Nieh was thinking, said "You have parents who are getting old, and though you have an older brother who can take care of them, I cannot tell you to stay, in case you may want to travel to study more. I have a disciple living on a certain mountain; if you go see him, give him a message for me, and also show him the Basic Book. Then you will be able to find out what it means. If you don't see him, just throw the Basic Book in the cave above a certain ravine, and scratch my message on a rock there. Then my disciple will teach you the essential Way himself."

After he had said this much, T'ung-hsiu sent Nieh back. All of a sudden Nieh found that T'ung-hsiu had disappeared, and he himself was near the place he had started from. He went back to the Observatory of Pure Space, where the Taoist priests said in astonishment that he had been gone for seven days. Where did he go?

Nieh told them the whole story, and two of the priests were so excited that they begged to go back with him. They did go, and when they reached the place where Nieh had been, the rock formations and vegetation were as he had seen them, but they could not find the reed house. They looked around all day in dismay and finally returned to the observatory.

Anyway, Nieh had the Basic Book, which was written in readable characters, telling about the true secret of the esoteric essentials used by the Queen Mother of the Celestial Court to order and educate the Community of Immortals. When those immortals put it into practice, they should attain the ability to ascend to heaven; when mortals in the world receive it, while on earth they participate in the Inner Government. There were some points, however, whose meaning eluded him, so he later went to the Observatory of Reality and stayed there for a month looking for traces of Hsieh T'ung-hsiu's disciple.

Some people said there was a hermit who lived around the ravine T'ung-hsiu had mentioned, but no one knew his name, though sometimes people saw him. Nieh went into the mountains time and time again looking for him, but did not see him. At length he did as T'ung-hsiu had told him, throwing the book into the cave and scratching the message on a rock face. After that he dreamed that a spiritual man named Purple Sacred Mushroom, the disciple of T'ung-hsiu, taught him in such a way that his mental blocks melted away. Then he awoke.

A year or more later, he again returned to his original hermitage on the mountain near his hometown, and lived there for over twenty years. He regarded the Real Humans T'sai, P'eng, and Hsieh as his occult mentors, and personally oversaw the collection of tales about these immortals from among the Taoist priests and the general populace.

Eventually Nieh Shih-tao was recognized as a Taoist adept of great powers, respected by all. His prayers were always answered, and he had over five hundred disciples, at least fifteen of whom also attained adepthood and graced the Mystic School. People came from all around to study with him, and he taught them according to their natures and perceptions. He died at the age of sixty-eight, but like many of the Real People was seen from time to time for years and years afterward.

Sayings of *Ancestor* Lü

INTRODUCTION

Lü Yen (Lü Yan), commonly known in folklore as Lü Tung-pin (Lü Dongbin), is also called Lü Tsu (Lü Zu), or "Ancestor Lü," in recognition of his place in Taoist history as a progenitor of the school of Complete Reality. In Taoist tradition he is believed to have lived in the T'ang dynasty (618–905 C.E.). Some sources place his birth as early as the year 646, but other materials suggest much later dates. He is one of the greatest figures of folk Taoism and esoteric Taoism alike, and an enormous body of literature is attributed to his spiritual inspiration. His own work, along with later writings ascribed to him, is particularly noteworthy for its integration of Confucianism and Buddhism with classical, religious, and alchemical Taoism.

Almost all of the writings and sayings attributed to Lü Yen are evidently products of mediums and other workers in the T'ien-hsien-p'a, or Sect of the Celestial Immortals, an offshoot of the Southern school of Complete Reality Taoism tracing its ancestry back through Lord Lü to the ancient Taoist schools of the Han and Chou dynasties. The present anthology contains works from both what would seem to be the original body of the writings of Ancestor Lü, who founded the Complete Reality school, and what are later developments in the literature of the Celestial Immortals Sect.

The sayings and writings translated in the present section are taken from the larger body of work deriving from the later activity of Lü's followers and the mediums of the Celestial Immortals Sect. They are particularly useful for the elegant simplicity with which they introduce the broad range of traditional teachings to which they are heir in a manner that makes the principles accessible to the lay person without sacrificing inner meaning.

The Three Treasures

The human body is only vitality, energy, and spirit. Vitality, energy, and spirit are called the three treasures. Ultimate sagehood and noncontrivance are both attained from these. Few people know these three treasures, even by way of their temporal manifestations. What is inconceivable is their primordial state—is it not lost? If you lose these three treasures, you are incapable of noncontrivance, and so are unaware of the primordial.

The Primordial

Not only is the primordial uncontrived, it has nothing to it that could be contrived. When you reach nonexistence of even uncontrivance, there is no nonexistence of noncontrivance, and so no nonexistence of nonexistence. This nonexistence of nonexistence is the primordial, yet the primordial contains everything. It is because there is the primordial that there is the temporal. The primordial of everything is one single primordial. The unique primordial is the primordial state of each thing, each individual, and thus it forms the temporal. Thus we get the three treasures. These three treasures are complete as a human being.

Vitality

In heaven, vitality is the Milky Way, it is the light of the sun, moon, and stars, it is rain and dew, sleet and hail, snow and frost. On earth it is water, streams, rivers, oceans, springs, wells, ponds, and marshes. In people it is vitality, the root of essence and life, the body of blood and flesh.

Energy

In heaven, energy is substance and form, yin and yang, the movement of the sun, moon, and stars, the processes of waxing and waning; it is clouds, mist, fog, and moisture; it is the heart of living beings, evolution and development. On earth, it is power, fuel, the pith of myriad beings, the source of mountain streams; it is lifegiving and killing, activating and storing; it is the passage of time, flourishing and decline, rising and falling, sprouts and sprout sheaths. In humans it is energy, physical movement, activity, speech, and perception; it is use of the body, the gateway of death and life.

Spirit

In heaven, spirit is the pivot, the true director, the silent mover; it is the essence of the sun, moon, and stars; it is the wind blowing, thunder pealing; it is compassion and dignity; it is the force of creation, the basis of the origin of beings. On earth, it is ability, communion, opening; it is the shapes of myriad species, mountains and waters; it is peace and quietude, the source of stability; it is calm, warmth, and kindness. In humans, it is the spirit, the light in the eyes, thought in the mind; it is wisdom and intelligence, innate knowledge and capacity; it is the government of vitality and energy, awareness and understanding; it is the basis of the physical shell, the foundation of the life span.

Stabilizing Vitality

The three treasures are not easily obtained. Since they are not easy to obtain, how can we not take care of them? They are to be taken care of, and this is accomplished by purity and tranquillity, not agitating the vitality, not letting it leak, so that it abides peacefully in its original home, true to reality as it is, circulating three hundred and sixty-one times in a day and night, returning to its original home, true to its own nature, immutable, forming the stabilizing ingredient of the elixir of immortality.

Guarding Energy

Vitality is always controlled by energy. Once energy runs outside, vitality eventually leaks out. Therefore, to stabilize vitality one should guard the energy. How is energy to be guarded? This requires freedom from craving, clear openness and serenity, not acting impulsively. The energy is to be placed in the mysterious pass, where it is brought to be nurtured and calmed. Always free, the energy is then unified, whole, unfragmented, all-pervasive, without gaps. After the energy is thus developed, it is brought down to merge with the vitality, unobstructed, like water and milk blending into one. Then the medicinal ingredients of the great elixir are naturally completed. Now just add the firing, and the effect will appear in the crucible.

Preserving Spirit

The firing is the spirit. Vitality cannot be concentrated except by energy, but vitality and energy cannot be operated without the spirit to stabilize the vitality, and nurturing the energy is just a matter of preserving the spirit. In the work of preserving the spirit, it is important to stop rumination, with nothing coming out from within and nothing coming in from outside. With all signs of emotion gone, one plunges into a state of boundlessness, lightness, blissful fluidity, tranquil independence.

Emergence of the Spirit

When the spirit is preserved in this way, it abides in its chamber. The chamber of the spirit is in the alchemical storehouse. Once the alchemical storehouse is firmly secured, the spirit is calm and collected: controlling and operating the vitality and energy, thereby it crystallizes the great elixir, which is in the form of an infant resembling oneself. This then emerges from the forehead to travel through the universe; in the interval of an exhalation and inhalation, it travels unhindered through the ten directions, inconceivably serene and content.

If you stick to this, however, and do not hear of the Great Way or meet Real People, you will be affected by three calamities. Then if you do not awaken, the accomplishment that has been achieved will all go to waste.

The Three Calamities

What are the three calamities? One is called the hard wind. The hard wind is sharp, cutting, and piercing; it enters through the forehead and penetrates the bones and joints, right down to the bottom of the feet. The limbs and hair fall apart, becoming wispy threads floating about loose.

If the hard wind cannot invade you, then there is a poisonous fire, which rises from below and enters through the top of the head, attacking the internal organs and burning the limbs. The pores and the hairline are instantly turned into ashes.

If your achievement is not harmed by this wind and fire, then it can be said to be consummate, unless you still have not learned the Way. Then there are five thunders, each with accompaniments, which circle and attack. As long as you have not learned the Great Way, the vital spirit will scatter in a moment, never to stabilize and unify.

Therefore it is imperative to study the Great Way, for if you do not study the Great Way you cannot escape these three calamities and will lose your three treasures. So it is only people of understanding who know this and therefore go in search of elevated Real People who will teach them the Great Way so that they can be forever free from the three calamities.

The Great Way

The Great Way is very difficult to express in words. Because it is hard to speak of, just look into beginninglessness, the beginningless beginning. When you reach the point where there is not even any beginninglessness, and not even any nonexistence of beginninglessness, this is the primordial. The primordial Way cannot be assessed; there is nothing in it that can be assessed. What verbal explanation is there for it? We cannot explain it, yet we do explain it—where does the explanation come from? The Way that can be explained is only in doing. What is doing? It is attained by nondoing. This nondoing begins in doing.

Doing

How is doing applied? To study its application, one must ask the autonomous mind. The autonomous mind is imbued with great understanding; it observes the changes of movement and stillness of yin and yang, looks to absolute yang and emulates its firm action, looks to absolute yin and communes with its process. The autonomous mind also studies the four seasons and models itself on their cycle. Silently comprehending the ultimate, it plumbs the original source.

Thus extensively observing all processes of creation and evolution, sitting calmly with the mind in trance, the energy of trance exists alone, calm sitting exists alone. Now there is nothing whatsoever in the autonomous mind, and the infant resembling the self that was previously cultivated and crystallized by the alchemical elixir communes with heaven and earth.

Transmission

It is necessary, however, to seek the guidance of elevated real people. If you do not meet real people who can point out the refinements and subtleties, you will not understand the Great Way. In that case, whatever you understand will still be superficial, and you will ultimately fail to attain the mysterious profundities. If you do not attain the profundities, how can you understand the Great Way? So we know that the Great Way requires us to seek true transmission.

This true transmission is received individually from a teacher; there is an opening up in the darkness, resulting in clear understanding. Once you are capable of clear understanding, you eventually realize the hidden mystery. Upon realizing the hidden mystery, you know the Great Way. This is called having knowledge and is regarded as attainment. When you attain this ultimate mystery, then nondoing is finally possible.

Undertakings and Worthy Deeds

Even if you have attained nondoing, you should still carry out undertakings, fulfilling them and realizing their proper results. After many undertakings, you should accomplish worthy deeds, fulfilling them completely and realizing their proper results.

Those whose worthy deeds are great realize great fruits of their causes; they may become incorruptible immortals and take their places in the ranks of the celestials, or they may remain in the human world as masters of all things, or they may live in a state of pure bliss.

Those whose worthy deeds rank next also lie in highest heaven as nondoing immortals, roaming in ecstasy, or they may live on special mountains, or they may travel in the polluted world as guides to the Way.

Those whose worthy deeds are shallow abide eternally in natural settings, among the springs and rocks, unborn and undying, forever free from the three calamities.

Some know that there is a distinct order in learning the Way. There is neither difficulty nor ease, but for the proper results look to deeds and undertakings; the deeds and undertakings accumulated each produce their proper results, but if you want the proper results you must learn the Great Way.

Order on the Way

If you want to learn the Great Way, you must value
the three treasures. Without the three treasures you
cannot live long, and deep attainment cannot be
reached in a limited time; so you will not learn the
Great Way. Without learning the Great Way there is
no purpose to accumulating deeds, so deeds thus
accumulated are not great achievements. If you immediately think of the elevated sages and thereupon
grasp the Great Way without establishing great
works or fulfilling great undertakings, it is as though
you have gained nothing.

Entering the Way

Observe what people who arrived did to enter the Way. They strove mightily, as if they feared they wouldn't reach it, and looked all over for elevated Real People to teach them the mysterious wonder. Plunged into danger, they were not cowed; plunged into difficulty, they were not disturbed; faced with obstacles, they were not confused; confronted with hardships that refined them, they had no regrets. Such was their sincerity that they moved the Real People to teach them the essential, and thus they were able to attain penetrating understanding, without distortion. Then they came back and sat, silently carrying on mystic work, gazing above and examining below, realizing the mystery of mysteries.

Yet they still did not become complacent: they mixed in with the ordinary world and carried out various undertakings and performed various deeds in the cities, towns, and villages. Thinking their works were still shallow, they made yet broader commitments, to carry out unlimited undertakings and accomplish unlimited deeds. They vowed that all people through the ages, those with knowledge and those without, would hear of the Great Way and ascend to the ultimate goal.

The Ultimate Goal

So this undertaking could not be finished even in ten million eons. If this were ever fully accomplished, it would be truly supreme, reaching nondoing, reaching to where there is not even any nondoing. This nondoing is coextensive with heaven and earth, but not coterminous. This is because both heaven and earth are created, and they consist of that which is created, so they must end. Because heaven does something, it too must suffer wastage. People who have arrived on the Way have no doing, and nondoing cannot suffer wastage or aging.

These ultimate people exist before heaven and earth exist, and emerge once heaven and earth come to exist. While heaven and earth wear out, these ultimate people are safe. This is very subtle indeed; I can hardly describe such ultimate people, but in the final analysis all people are like this. How are they like this? Because of the primordial. The primordial is inherent in everyone.

The Primordial and the Acquired

People have the primordial, but are mostly unaware of it. What is the reason for this? It is because while there is the primordial, there is also the acquired. Since there is that which is temporally acquired, there are six organs of sense. Once there are sense organs, they produce six consciousnesses.

What are the six organs? One is the eye; this eye organ looks at color and form and produces various states of mind that obscure the primordial. Another is the ear; this organ listens to sounds and produces various states of mind that obscure the primordial. Another is the mouth, which utters judgments that produce various states of mind that obscure the primordial. Another is the nose; this organ smells odors and produces various states of mind that obscure the primordial. Another is the tongue; this organ tastes flavors and produces various states of mind that obscure the primordial. Another is the body; this experiences situations and produces various states of mind that obscure the primordial.

Therefore these six organs are called the six robbers. If you want to learn the Great Way, first remove the six organs. As long as the six organs are not removed, they produce wrong consciousness.

Removing the Six Organs

How are the six organs removed? In ancient times there were adepts who knew the way to remove them. They did not dwell on any objects of sense: they saw without using their eyes, heard without using their ears, shut their mouths and withdrew their tongues, being like imbeciles all day long. They breathed from their heels, set their bodies aside unused, and performed all actions by the operation of the spirit. In this way the six organs were all there, yet it was as if they did not exist.

If one does not have the six organs, how can bad tendencies arise? There being no such tendencies of consciousness, as a result there is no obstruction. There being no obstruction, the mind is at peace. With the mind thus free from defilement and attachment, you set up the furnace and put in the three treasures; they can crystallize the great elixir, because that is what is produced by their conjunction.

Making the Elixir

Using real knowledge, harmony, and awareness, combine them with the three treasures. When the three become one, the great elixir is made. Once you have made the great elixir, essence and sense submit, and the earthly and celestial are in their places. It is necessary, however, to seek elevated Real People to indicate to you the hidden subtleties in order that the proper results be attained.

Malpractice

Lesser people do not know the basis and so act out erroneous ideas. They carry out various deviant practices, turning further and further away from the Way. Because of this aberration, they are beset by various bedevilments and obstacles. They incur the anger of heaven above and violate civil laws below.

If they take to seclusion, addicted to natural settings, as they know about the aforementioned type, they refine their energy and tranquilize the spirit, gathering the three treasures in hopes of producing the great elixir. But if they do not obtain directions in genuine method, ultimately they will be afflicted by the three calamities.

Dissipation

The human body is only vitality, energy, and spirit. If you do not care about your vitality and waste it arbitrarily, that is like putting water into a leaking cup; it will not fill the cup, but will gradually leak away. Finally it will be all gone, not a drop left. If you do not care about your energy but let it go whichever way it will, that is like placing incense on a red-hot brazier, letting it burn away; add more fuel and fire, and the incense will become ash. If you do not care about your spirit and dissipate it arbitrarily, that is like placing a lone lamp in the wind, letting it be blown by the wind, uncovered, so that it goes out.

The Seed of Emotions

Because of the six organs, people produce the six consciousnesses; and because of the six consciousnesses they produce emotions. They hardly realize that emotions confuse them in regard to fundamental reality. Once fundamental reality is lost sight of, then emotions run wild. But the seed of all emotions is craving. Why is this? Because craving is at the root of emotions. If you don't crave anything, you don't want anything; if you don't want anything, how can you be attracted to anything? If you are not attracted to anything, you are not repulsed by anything; if you have neither attraction nor repulsion, what anger can there be? When there is no anger, fear does not occur; without fear, sadness disappears.

So we know that craving is the root of emotions. If you try to control emotions forcibly without extirpating the root, you control nothing but outgrowths. This is like a flood of water: if you try to dam it without stopping the source or clearing the flow, eventually you'll be drowned. It is also like a blazing fire: if you try to beat it out without removing its fuel or cutting off its path, you'll just increase the force of the flames, so that you'll be threatened at every turn. It is also like the waves of the ocean, one following another endlessly.

Feeling emotions and evoking them, they all accompany the mind, growing according to circumstances. Only developed people, knowing the seed, use the sword of wisdom with great aspiration and fierce determination to cut through the root and sprouts, extirpate undesirable syndromes, and prevent emotions from growing on them like parasites.

Disorientation

The emotions are a huge bolt, and craving is the lock on the bolt. When you cut through the lock and take away the bolt, you can get beyond the barrier and go in peace, freely, without hindrance. Mastering understanding of the ultimate Way, you then ascend to exalted reality. I pity people who create all sorts of demons and obstacles because of craving. They are confused and disoriented all their lives, rarely taking stock of themselves. Even when people of high attainment try to enlighten them, it is like beating a drum for the deaf, like presenting a lamp to the blind. After all they do not wake up. What a pity! Still they feign interest in the Way, but their interest is misguided—what they seek is immortality. This is like opening Pandora's box—it's not that they don't find anything, but there is harm in it.

Removing Emotions

How can you remove emotions? The way to remove them is to think there is no self. What is called no self? The self is originally not self; we are not these selves. So what does the self cleave to? Once there is self and you cling to it as yourself, when clinging to the self as yourself, then nothing is not self. When nothing is not self, there is nothing to which the self does not cleave. The country is not one's own, yet one will die for love of it; the home is not one's own, yet one will die for love of it. Things are not one's own, yet one dies for them, like flies seeking ordure, like ants gathering in putrid flesh, like bees trying to get through a closed window, smashing themselves against it when they see the sunlight. Gluttony and greed make people like vultures, insatiably voracious. But try to think of the self; before the self existed, it wasn't like this: it must have been clear and cool. The self is transient, like a fleeting shadow, like the morning dew—in a moment the self is gone. Since the self has no self, what is the purpose of self-love? You will grab your heart and laugh in astonishment; when you meditate in this way, what craving will not disappear?

Detachment

Once craving is eliminated, everything will disappear—desire, aversion, attraction, sorrow, fear, anger, ego, emotion. All will end with this craving. But people stick to craving as though they have fallen into an abyss. Though they try to swim out, there is no shore. What is needed first is patience, which means that you should think to yourself and reflect with increasing intensity.

In ancient times there was a rich man with many wives and children, surrounded by every luxury. One day he lost everything dear to him, and his mind was impressed with the Way. At this point he was surrounded by demons calling to him enticingly, trying to hold him back, taunting him, weeping, encircling and embracing him, not letting him go free. But this high-minded man remained patient and unconcerned. He looked upon what he had lost as like a broken pot, like worn-out shoes. Quietly disappearing into the mountains, stilling his breath and plunging into profound silence, not seeing or hearing anything, he caused his mind to be entirely free of emotion, vastly expanded, open and empty.

Yet when one has reached this stage, it is still necessary to go into the ordinary world with all its clamor and toil, experience all kinds of situations, observe all sorts of phenomena, and become familiar with people. When you can roam playfully, going in and out of the world without becoming influenced or attached, then you humbly seek the secret of the mysterious pass and refine the three treasures.

Governing the Mind

Since the refinement of the three treasures requires removal of emotions, it is necessary to govern the mind. What is governing the mind? The mind is originally pure, the mind is originally calm; openness and freedom are both basic qualities of mind. When we govern the mind, this means we should keep it as it is in its original fundamental state, clear as a mountain stream, pure, fresh, unpolluted, silent as an immense canyon, free from clamor, vast as the universe, immeasurable in extent, open as a great desert, its bounds unknown.

In this way, the mind with nothing in it is like charcoal or still water: charcoal can burn, still water can reflect. It may also be likened to a clear mirror, with no images in it once objects are gone. It is also like enlightenment, constituting the root of the Way. When the clear mirror is always polished and enlightenment is refreshed from time to time, the clear mirror is cold, and the heart of enlightenment leaves its impression. Being cold means all objects disappear; when the heart leaves its impression, all paths arise.

Sitting Forgetting

I know without knowing, see without seeing; I have no ears, no eyes, no mind, no thought, no cognition. Thus having nothing, then reaching absence of even nothingness, after that the mind cannot be disturbed by anything. Being imperturbable is called sitting forgetting.

Once you can forget, you can be given the Way. You can thus pass through the barriers, tame essence and sense, establish the foundation of enlightenment and make it accessible to consciousness. If, however, in forgetting things you can battle with things but cannot settle them, and you seek to learn the secrets of the Way in this condition, it will not only be of no benefit, it will even be harmful.

The Chief Hoodlum

To learn the Way we first kill off the chief hoodlum. What is the chief hoodlum? It is emotions. We need to wipe out that den of thieves to see once again the clear, calm, wide open original essence of mind. Don't let conditioned senses spy in.

What is this about? It is about quelling the mind. One removes emotions to quell the mind, then purifies the mind to nurture its great elixir.

Essence

Some people practice aberrant techniques that not only obscure the Way but also obscure their own essence. Essence is that which is bestowed by Nature. Therefore quelling the mind is done for the sake of this essence. When the mind is surely quelled, how can essence be obscured?

So the effort to nurture essence is not to be relaxed. How is essence to be nurtured? This essence is rooted in the beginningless, espied in the absolute, and becomes fragmented in the temporal.

In the temporally conditioned essence there is inner design and energy. Inner design is divided into real and false; the false has lost the natural reality. Energy is divided into pure and polluted; the polluted is murky, and being murky and degraded cannot be called essence any more but is called temporally acquired conditioning.

The Absolute

In the absolute, inner design and energy are whole and integrated; there is nothing false, and no pollution. This is the celestial state of nature. Now when it comes to the beginningless, we cannot say it is essence and cannot say it is life; it being neither essence nor life, how can we say nature is rooted in the beginningless? We must realize that the beginningless is neither essence nor life, it is a seed in the absolute void. This seed becomes the root of the ultimate, whereupon there is life and essence. To nurture this essence is to nurture this seed.

Nurturing the Seed

The seed of the beginningless is undefinable, imperceptible, formless; how does one set about nurturing it? The way to nurture it is to nurture the temporal first. The temporal nature has inner design and energy, pure and polluted, real and false, which cannot be equated; what can be nurtured? Nurturing and quelling means to get rid of the false and purify the polluted. Getting rid of the false is not easy, purifying the polluted is difficult. Out of pity for people, I will point out the way to start.

Where do you start? From pure desirelessness. When you have no desire, there is reality. Reality is without fabrication; when there is no fabrication, there is purity. When pure, you can be clear; when real, you can understand. What can you clearly understand? The attainment of pure reality illumines everything; the clarity of illumination understands every way.

Removing Falsehood and Pollution

How are falsehood and pollution removed? On the lower terrestrial plane, falsehood and pollution are mixed together; therefore I will give directions. It is necessary to be buoyant, to rise on high, making a profound effort to avoid entanglement in worldly objects. Sit in deep tranquillity with eyes downcast. Do not see, do not hear, and the mind will be clear and calm, without any garbage in it. After that you can get rid of falsehood and clean away acquired pollution. Once acquired pollution is cleared away, the mind is pure and no externals can adhere to it.

Mastering Mind

In order to master the mind it is necessary to banish five kinds of consciousness, thereby get rid of five obstacles, and thus understand five natures and penetrate five mysteries.

Causeless Consciousness

When people sit quietly in total stillness, with no images appearing to them, their ears not receiving anything, their eyes not making contact with anything, in a state of profound silence, undifferentiated, with steadily concentrated awareness, it may happen that suddenly a thought arises, drawing forth an outburst like wild animals galloping in all directions, out of control. This is very harmful to the Way, so students of the Way first get rid of this kind of consciousness. Where does this consciousness come from, and how does one get rid of it? The way to get rid of it is to eliminate falsehood and maintain truthfulness.

Consciousness of the Future

Before situations have been experienced, before matters arise, you should make your mind clear and calm. Clarity and calm are roots of the Way, but it can happen that you may for no reason get caught up in all sorts of before-the-fact considerations, assailed by a hundred thoughts; then when you go through situations, dealing with people and events, they turn out differently than you thought, and so you try to make your thoughts fit them. This depletes the vitality, wearies the spirit, and exhausts the energy. It is better not to be conscious of the future, letting it be as it may. Therefore students who do not get rid of this consciousness can hardly learn the Way. The way to get rid of this consciousness is to forget objects, dismiss concerns, and clear the mind so that it is like space.

Consciousness of Sound and Form

What the ear hears and what the eye sees may be beautiful or ugly, fair or foul, may have any of a countless variety of features. You view them subjectively, like dreams, yet you do not understand this and become actually attached to them. First conscious of what is pleasing and displeasing, you devise strategies, uneasy and anxious, agitated and restless, so the luminous essence of mind is covered by shadows and you become feebleminded, unable to attain clarity. How can you study the great Way in this condition? You will on the contrary destroy yourself.

Therefore students of the Way silence the superficial intellect and cause the inner mind to be ever alert, realizing that if this consciousness remains it produces affliction, with no prospect of getting out of the confusion caused by affliction, anxious and insecure. When the autonomous mind emerges, it will get rid of this, clearly aware, free from entanglement or dependence, thoroughly equanimous outwardly and inwardly. Using ears for eyes and eyes for ears, no matter how extreme the situation may be, you do not see or hear.

Consciousness of the Past

Whether there is good or bad fortune, if feelings are forgotten along with situations, what gain or loss is there, what weakness or strength? The ignorant are bound up in many concerns, upset and uneasy, confused and worried, going mad by losing their minds for no reason. To try to comprehend the Way in this condition is like trying to cross the ocean in a tub, leaving you helplessly adrift; it is like trying to descend into an abyss of a thousand fathoms by means of a well rope, which is not only impossible but dangerous. Therefore students of the Way must clear away this consciousness and not be fixated by it, so that nothing retards them and they are in a state of wholeness, everything evaporating, leaving no more false awareness mixing up true awareness.

Consciousness of Personal Knowledge

Considering oneself to be intelligent and enlightened is not going by the right Way. Unaware that presumption of personal knowledge greatly obstructs the Way, you go back and forth in a fog, stagnant, without expanding. This not only obstructs the Way, it actually destroys essential life. Therefore students of the Way work to eliminate this consciousness, because if they do not eliminate this consciousness they will never clarify true consciousness even if they eliminate other consciousnesses.

The Level Road

The Great Way is like a level road. If you do not proceed to traverse the level road by way of true consciousness, you fall into sidetracks. When people get mixed up in any of the countless cults, even if they are admonished they can rarely wake up, and even if there is true guidance they do not follow it. Even if causeless consciousness, consciousness of the future, consciousness of sound and form, and consciousness of the past are all forgotten, still if the consciousness of personal knowledge is kept you will be lost after all.

Spontaneity

Serenely accord with spontaneity; don't act willfully, or you'll lose the fundamental. What is the fundamental? It is the essence of mind. The awareness in this essence is called true awareness. The awareness of true awareness is called accurate awareness. The awareness of accurate awareness is great awareness. This great awareness is primal awareness; it doesn't depend on calculation or reasoning, it is not willful, insistent, fixated, or egotistic. If you follow its basic truth and let it be as it spontaneously is, then you will understand the beginningless and endless, penetrating the universe.

This is very subtle and abstruse. Taoists call it the knowledge of sages, Confucians call it spiritual communication, Buddhists call it silent illumination. These are all terms for true awareness, accurate awareness, great awareness, primal awareness. Consciousness without this awareness is called false consciousness. Unless false consciousness is eliminated, it will obscure true awareness.

But to eliminate false consciousness, it is best to get rid of five obstacles.

Bedevilment

The obstacle of bedevilment may arise in the mind, may attach to objects, may operate through other people, or may pertain to the body. Bedevilments arising in the mind are ideas of self and others, ideas of glory and ignominy, ideas of gain and loss, ideas of right and wrong, ideas of profit and honor, ideas of superiority. These are dust on the pedestal of the spirit, preventing freedom.

Bedevilment in the body is when it is invaded by illness, hunger, cold, satiation, pain and pleasure; when one becomes comfortable, one becomes lazy, repeating vicious circles into which one becomes trapped and bound. There is disharmony in action, which carries over into the way one deals with situations. There are both pleasant and unpleasant situations: the pleasant are considered easy, the unpleasant are considered difficult. To enter the world is easy, to leave the world is hard; when confronted with fine things, then jealousy, willfulness, and attraction take over.

Everyone has such bedevilments; if students of the Way do not get rid of this obstacle, they will never be able to learn the Way. So get rid of these obstructing bedevilments one by one.

Doubt

What is the obstacle of doubt? The Great Way is easy
to know, simple to do; the indications of an illumined teacher are a lamp in a dark room, bright and
clear, like a crystal globe. Nevertheless, the obstacle
of doubt plants its roots. When one person talks
about the Way, many people add their remarks and
opinions, until the influence of the clamor becomes
blinding, and people turn from that which is accurate to that which is deviant, confusing the true
with the false. This is like falling off a tree into a
deep canyon.

The words of the sages are supreme indeed: "The
open spirit does not die; it is the entry to all mar-
vels." The Way of the sages is great indeed: open and
free, responding to cause, pure and serene. What is
the use of different doctrines? Arbitrary indulgence
in fuss and confusion makes the obstacle of doubt,
by which people impede themselves. What a pity
that they do not understand and wind up subject to
pernicious influences.

It is necessary for practitioners to learn from genuine teachers; don't be confused by false doctrines, and don't take to sidetracks. Clear openness, calm stability, nurturing vitality, nurturing spirit, the mysterious pass, mystic receptivity, pure attention, nascent enlightenment, yin and yang, real knowing and conscious knowing, overcoming pitfalls, illumination, creative strength and receptive tranquillity—all are in the mind. What is the use of names? Forms do not remain. It is so simple and easy—what doubt is there? If you do not get rid of the obstacle of doubt, there will be a thicket of confusion.

The Obstacle of Principle

Even when the obstacle of doubt is removed, there is still the obstacle of principle, which is even more harmful to the Way. The obstacle caused by individual clinging to partiality prevents comprehensive perception. The obstacle of Confucians is in reification, the obstacle of Taoists is in nothingness, and the obstacle of Buddhists is in emptiness.

Reification

Those obstructed by reification cling to their partial principle; while they act in illusory situations, deal with illusory affairs, and see illusory persons, they take them all to actually exist. They belabor their minds, wear out their bodies, and exhaust their energy, considering all this obligatory in principle, unaware that these ideas are obstacles.

Now in human life, benevolence, duty, kindness, generosity, loyalty, respect, restraint, and vigor are all the abundant energy of heaven and earth; they are to be practiced genuinely and should not be considered vain. If the principles one observes are not fully digested, however, and one clings only to partial principles, then this will degenerate into a bad cause.

Sentimental benevolence, ostentatious dutifulness, petty loyalty, and ignorant respectfulness are criticized even in Confucianism, to say nothing of Taoism. It is lamentable how people are obstructed by reification; they fall into a pit of fire, without real understanding.

The psychological certitude of sages is comprehended and penetrated by silent recognition and thorough investigation; there is nothing idle in it at all.

Nothingness

Those obstructed by nothingness, clinging one-sidedly to this principle, sit blankly to clear away sense objects and think that the Way is herein. None of them seeks the secret of nurturing the three treasures. Though they speak of reaching nothingness, this is really not the Way. The ultimate Way is not in reification, nor simple nothingness. The mystic essential is to balance openness and realism.

Emptiness

Those obstructed by emptiness cling to this partial principle; not knowing true essence, they vainly talk of empty emptiness, and emptiness is not voided, so it becomes nihilistic emptiness. Ultimately they are unaware of the independence of original true suchness.

Sectarianism

All those obstructed by the three obstacles of reification, nothingness, and emptiness are unable to reconcile the three teachings of Confucianism, Taoism, and Buddhism. This results in sectarian differences and disputes. Confucians criticize the nothingness of Taoism, Taoists criticize the emptiness of Buddhism, Buddhists criticize the path of Confucianism—and so it goes on endlessly, back and forth. They do not realize that the basis is really one, even though the doctrines may be different. Their perception is divisive because they are obstructed by their principles.

Integration

The obstacle of reification leads to delusion, which makes it hard to wake up. The obstacle of nothingness leads to withering, in which there is no realism. The obstacle of emptiness leads to quietism, which reverts to nihilism. The ancient sages were realistic yet open, empty yet realistic. They saw that emptiness is not empty, that emptiness does not void anything. This is the supreme Way. It is attained by integration. It is only because of succumbing to the obstacle of principle that no one knows this. So students of the Way should be careful.

The Obstacle of Writings

For the obstacle of principle to be removed, there is an obstacle whose roots derive from writings. But in reality, the obstacle of writings is an obstacle of mind. The mystic sayings of the *Tao-te Ching* all come from profound enlightenment: if you view them literally and lose their inner sense, if you fail to understand and succumb to this obstacle, then all sorts of false statements, aberrated doctrines, curiosities, and fantasies enter your mind, causing damage to the nature and body.

So what ancient adepts set up as truths were mostly in the form of indirect allusions. For example, the terms water and fire, furnace and cauldron, girl and boy, dragon and tiger, yin and yang, and mysterious female—all are allusions to something else. People who are obstructed by words often do exercises without knowing the Great Way is in vitality, energy, and spirit. Nurturing these three treasures is nurturing the seed; this seed is the root of the ultimate. What all those terms refer to is this one energy; the basis of the energy is this seed.

When you recognize the seed, all the various explanations are dregs. Why consume the dregs?

So writings are not real explanations of the Way. When you personally realize the Way, you can dispense with all the writings.

The Obstacle of Tradition

If you do away with writings but still stick to a teacher's tradition, this very teacher's tradition becomes a source of obstruction. You should by all means examine clearly and go to visit adepts who can transmit the profound marvel. If you don't find such a person, you will suffer from obstruction all your life. Generally speaking, beginners have dreams about the Way; once they make a mistake in choosing a teacher and are given false teachings, they are confused and cannot attain enlightenment. They follow false teachings all their lives, thinking them true guidance. Their bodies and minds become imprisoned, so that even if real people point out true awakening to them, they may repudiate it and turn away. Once they have tasted fanciful talk, they sell falsehood by falsehood, believe falsehood through falsehood. All sorts of obstructions arise from this.

Therefore students of the Way should be careful to choose high illuminates, to get rid of obstructions of body and mind. When these obstacles are eliminated, all obstructions disappear. Once obstructions dissolve, the spiritual base is clear and clean; then one can be given explanation of the subtleties of the five natures.

Five Natures

The earthy nature is mostly turbid, and the turbid are mostly dull. The metallic nature is mostly decisive, and the decisive are mostly determined. The wooden nature is mostly kind, and the kind are mostly benevolent. The fiery nature is mostly adamant, and the adamant are mostly manic. The watery nature is mostly yielding, and the yielding are mostly docile.

The docile tend to wander aimlessly. The manic tend to undergo extremes. The benevolent tend to harmonize warmly. The determined tend to be strong and brave. The dull tend to be closed in.

The closed-in are ignorant; the strong and brave are unruly; those who wander aimlessly are shifty; those who harmonize warmly fall into the traps; those who are adamant and can endure extremes are cruel.

Therefore each of the five natures has a bias, so it is important to balance each with the others. By yielding one can overcome being adamant, by being adamant one can overcome yielding. Benevolence is balanced by effectiveness, effectiveness is balanced benevolence. The ignorance of earthy dullness is to be overcome by developed understanding. If developed understanding is not dominant, one loses the function of yielding.

Those who are too yielding tend to be lazy. Those who are too benevolent are foolish, and being foolish tend to be blind. Those who are too adamant tend to be rebellious. Those who are too determined tend to be stubborn. Those who are too dull do not have clear understanding and become alienated from reality.

Balanced Personality

In terms of social virtues, the water nature corresponds to wisdom, the fire nature corresponds to courtesy, the wood nature corresponds to benevolence, the metal nature corresponds to righteousness, and the earth nature corresponds to trustworthiness. In a balanced personality, these five natures should be able to produce and control one another.

Wisdom should be able to produce benevolence. Benevolence should be able to produce courtesy. Courtesy should be able to produce trustworthiness. Trustworthiness should be able to produce righteousness. Righteousness should be able to produce wisdom.

Wisdom should control courtesy. Courtesy should control righteousness. Righteousness should control benevolence. Benevolence should control trustworthiness. Trustworthiness should control wisdom.

When these five natures produce and control each other thus in a continuous circle, then no element of personality dominates; they all interact, balancing each other, resulting in completeness of the five natures.

Those who know this truly understand the ultimate design; then when they are told of the subtleties of the five mysteries, they can understand them on their own.

The Five Mysteries

The five mysteries are the mystery of heaven, the mystery of earth, the mystery of natural law, the mystery of the Way, and the total mystery of mysteries.

When you penetrate the mystery of heaven, then you know the course of heaven; emulating its spontaneity, you can be uncontrived. When you penetrate the mystery of earth, then you know the pattern of earth; emulating its firmness and flexibility, you can master balanced interaction. When you penetrate the mystery of natural law, you know cause and response, and assess unexpected changes before they become apparent. When you penetrate the mystery of the Way, then you comprehend the subtleties of the temporal and the primordial, of doing and nondoing; this is penetration of the mystery of mysteries.

Heaven above, earth below, the natural law of the Way, the refined and the profound—you will then know them all. You know, yet have no knowledge; and still there is nothing you do not know. Knowing all events but really having no knowledge is called attaining the Way.

The Mystery of Heaven

The deep blue of heaven spreads all over; it has shape but is not shape, has form but is not form. Its shape and form have a certain appearance; this is called substantiality. Yet that appearance is vague and ungraspable; substantiality has no definite form, but is open and traceless, and can only be called empty.

Only by emptiness can one be aware, only by substantiality can one cover all. Now empty, now substantial, changing most marvelously, is that whereby one penetrates the mystery of heaven. When you know how to be both empty and substantial, there is no congestion; emulating nature, you work and adapt at will, in a comprehensive cycle that never ceases. Then the great elixir of life is made.

The Mystery of Earth

Earth is thick, broad, boundless. Insofar as it is empty above and substantial below, myriad beings are born from it; insofar as it is substantial above and empty below, myriad beings return to the root. Now empty, now substantial, it lasts forever with heaven. Its body is still, its function flows; mountains manifest its wonderful substance, rivers reveal its spirit.

By its substance it supports being, by its spirit it gathers consciousnesses. Without spirit there is no substance, without substance there is no spirit. Spirit is active, substance receptive; substance acts through spirit. Emptiness and substantiality interact and balance each other, subtly combining into one whole.

Taoists who master understanding of this principle combine the qualities of firmness and flexibility; as emptiness and substantiality produce one another, they penetrate the mystery of earth. Also, by understanding the basis of this, creativity and receptivity are established in their proper places, and the great elixir of life is made.

The Mystery of the Way

The mystery of the Way is not explained by words. If you consider it substantial, still all substance is empty. If you consider it empty, still all emptiness is substantial. If you want to talk about its alternating and interacting emptiness and substantiality, where does the substantiality exist, where is the emptiness clarified?

The substantiality within emptiness cannot be called substantial, the emptiness within substantiality cannot be called empty. Substantiality is not to be considered substantial, emptiness is not to be considered empty; yet though they are not to be considered empty or substantial, ultimately they are not nonexistent. Now empty, now substantial, it is difficult to express in words. Now empty, now substantial—it is subtle indeed.

Though you cannot consider it empty, it really is empty; though you cannot consider it substantial, it really is substantial. It cannot be called alternating emptiness and substantiality, yet it is really none other than alternating emptiness and substantiality.

Ultimate indeed is the mystery of the Way! It has no name or form. So profound are its depths that it is difficult to fathom. Therefore if you understand this mystery, the elixir of life is thoroughly refined.

The Mystery of Natural Law

The mystery of natural law is learned from a teacher, but it is based on the celestial order, which circulates throughout the earth. Once the Great Way is accomplished, then miracles, at the extreme end of natural law, are manifested at will, and supernatural powers are unfathomable. Then sky and earth are like a pouch, sun and moon are in a pot, the minuscule is gigantic, the macrocosm is minute; you can manipulate the cosmos at will, looking upon the universe as a mote of dust. Now integrating, now vanishing, now detached, now present, you enter the hidden and emerge in the evident; space itself disappears. You can even employ spirits and ghosts and make thunder and lightning.

You might call this emptiness, but there is nothing it doesn't contain; you might call this substantiality, but nothing in it really exists. When you attain it in the mind, activity corresponds; mind and activity reflect each other. The mind has no such mind; nothing is added by action. It is not attained in action, but operates in accord with the mind, changing unpredictably like a dream. Heaven and earth are the witnesses; it is most subtle, endlessly creative. Only when you penetrate the mystery of the Way do you then arrive at this essence; thereby you penetrate the mystery of natural law, and then the Way is completed.

The Mystery of Mysteries

There is no way to explain the mystery of mysteries in words, for it is even beyond thought. It is very subtle, ungraspable, extremely rarefied. From heaven up to the infinite heaven there are perfected people, most mysterious, by whom heaven is directed and earth controlled. They understand people and things, the hidden and the obvious, to the furthest possible extent. They operate time without any fixed track, and are invisibly in charge of the accounting of the ages. Sages cannot recognize them as sages, spirits cannot recognize them as spirits.

The mystery of mysteries is nonexistent, yet exists; it is empty, yet substantial. It is not more in sages, not less in the ignorant. Heaven is within it, yet even heaven does not know it; earth receives its current, yet even earth does not recognize it. It penetrates the depths of all things, yet they go on unaware. Its presence is not presence, its passing is not passing. How can this mystery of mysteries be conceived of, how can it be imagined? If you penetrate the essence, it is mystery upon mystery.

Learned Ignorance

In the absence of understanding, all sorts of different arguments, opinions, and theories arise, resulting in different schools and sects that each hold on to one point and repudiate others. Stubbornly holding on to their theories, they attack and goad each other; each maintaining one view, they argue and assert their own doctrines. They all want to be protectors of the Way, but though they speak out, they go to extremes.

The mind that understands the Way is entirely impartial and truthful. But because Taoist tradition has gone on so long, personalistic degenerations have cropped up. People attack one another and establish factions of supporters; they call themselves guardians of the Way, but they are really in it for their own sakes. When you look into their motivations, you find they are all outsiders. People like this are rot in Confucianism, bandits in Taoism, troublemakers in Buddhism. They are confused and obsessed.

A Dayfly

Human life in the world is no more than that of a dayfly. This is true not only of ordinary people but also of the wizards and buddhas of all times as well. However, though a lifetime is limited, the spirit is unlimited. If we look on the universe from the point of view of our lifetime, our lifetimes are those of dayflies. But if we look on the universe from the point of view of our spirit, the universe too is like a dayfly.

High Minds

People should have lofty vision and broad minds.
They should be hesitant to accept favor and patient
in ignominy. With a capacity vast as the ocean, a
mind open as space, if they are to receive much they
should do so without considering it glorious, and if
they should refuse something small they should do
so without making excuses. Ancient sages ruled
without taking it personally, or even abandoned
rulership like a worn-out shoe. When did they ever
keep wealth or poverty on their minds? Nowadays
many people tie up their minds with such thoughts,
unable to change. If some day they should be given
high rank and a large salary, I don't know what they
would be like.

Mothers

A woman carries a child in the womb for ten months, then gives birth in pain. Breast-feeding for three years, she watches over the infant with great care, aware of when it is sick, in pain, uncomfortable, itching. Whatever she does, even when she is not there, she always thinks of the baby. She is happy when she sees it laugh and worries when it cries. Seeing it stand and walk, she is at once anxious and exhilarated. She will go hungry to feed her child, she will freeze to clothe it. She watches, worries, and works, all for the child's future. How can one ever repay the debt one owes to one's mother?

Fathers

Fathers should not be too indulgent, nor be too strict. Only when there are wise fathers are there good children. Only when there are kind fathers are there respectful children. How many people could ever become talented without teaching, act on their own without encouragement, gain a sense of purpose without study? Fathers should be aware of this.

Good Deeds

Don't be concerned about whether merit in helpful deeds is great or small, much or little. Just be completely sincere. Then if you save even one insect, or care for one plant or tree, doing whatever you can, there is immeasurable merit in this.

Stable Perception

People's minds need stable perception. If the mind is unstable, you cannot apply it usefully to the realm of true enlightenment. Eventually you will become biased and opinionated and will not believe good words. Craftily employing mental tricks, contesting against others, unwilling to tame the crazy mind and return it to unity, you will be out of harmony with true enlightenment. As a result, though there be some good in what you do from time to time, since the mind is the root, if the root is defective a little goodness won't help.

Those who have this affliction should endeavor to change. Do not flaunt personal knowledge, do not cling to biased views. Purify your mind through and through, so there is no obstruction or attachment; act with all your heart. People of true enlightenment perform deeds of true enlightenment. Going higher with every step, wherever they go there is profit. To seek this in yourself, just fully exert your own sincerity. All the sages are ultimately one; once you understand, you receive blessings without end.

The True Eternal Tao

Whenever I see those whom the vulgar call devotees of the Tao, I find that all of them seek to be taken in by spirits and immortals, or they seek lasting life and preservation of wealth by the practice of material alchemy or sexual yoga. When it comes to the great Tao of true eternity, pure and open, tranquil and dispassionate, there are few who are interested in it.

Entering the Tao

The Tao is entered by way of sincerity. When you reach complete sincerity, the Tao is not far off. Therefore a classic says, "Before practicing the way of immortality, first practice the way of humanity."

What does practicing the way of humanity mean? The Tao is fundamentally empty, yet it fills the universe. People should embody the Tao in action, making the extent of their minds reach everywhere and encompass everything, so that all living creatures are embraced within the mind of the individual.

Also one should investigate the root of consciousness and the nature of intelligence, from time to time looking inward and using the mind to ask the mind whether one's actions are in accord with truth, and whether one is really contributing positively to society.

Life and Death

People usually fear death, but when they become seriously ill they long for a quick death to relieve them of their misery, and when they are utterly exhausted in a perilous situation they want to die quickly to escape their suffering. When you look at life and death in reverse this way, you break right through the mental block.

Restoring the Mind

To restore the mind to its unfragmented origin, sit quietly and meditate. First count the breaths, then tune the breath until it is imperceptible. Sense the body as like the undifferentiated absolute, and you won't hear anything. Those who can regain their composure after a mountain crumbles before them are second best; not even being startled is expertise.

A Temporary Device

As long as there is any thought left unterminated, one's essence is not whole. As long as the breath is even slightly unsettled, one's life is not secure. It is necessary to reach the point where mind and breath rest on each other, and thoughts are forgotten in the midst of thought. In essence it requires relaxation and patience. The secret is put this way: "No need to stay by the furnace and watch the firing. Just settle spirit and breath, and trust nature. When exhalation and inhalation stop and the body is as though dead, you will realize meditation is just a temporary device."

Joyfulness

One should not be happy or delighted when the spiritual work takes effect, for when the mind is delighted the energy floats up and one becomes greedy. When sitting meditating, joyfulness in the mind is the blooming of the mind blossom—it is best to nurture it.

States

As for the states experienced through the exercise of quiescence, first there is dullness, oblivion, and random thought. Then there is lightness and freshness. Later it is like being inside curtains of gold mesh. Finally it is like returning to life from death, a clear breeze under the bright moon coming and going, the scenery unobstructed.

Not Hearing

As for the exercise of sitting until one does not hear, at the extreme of quiet stillness, the mind is not drawn into movement by the ears. One hears only sound, not tone. This is not hearing.

Three Levels of Attainment

There are three levels of attainment of the Tao. One is the alchemy of nondoing. Another is the alchemy of spiritual power. The third is the alchemy of preserving unity.

In the alchemy of nondoing, the mind is the crucible. The intent is the fire. Walking, standing, sitting, and reclining are the laboratory. Joy, anger, sadness, and happiness are the firing process. Humanity, justice, loyalty, and truthfulness are culling and ingesting the elixir. Spring, summer, autumn, and winter are extraction and addition. Essence and sense are the medicinal ingredients.

In this alchemy, a month is condensed into a day, and the elixir takes one year to refine. When you use it all your life, you go beyond the heavens, leave being, and enter nonbeing. This is the method of unsurpassed true adepts, in which myriad practices are completely fulfilled. Tranquil, open, empty, mystery of mysteries, one joins the ancestor of heaven and earth. Working for the benefit of all people, participating in evolution, one joins the origin of heaven and earth. Even before the achievement is complete, the humane heart is universal; even before the virtue is consummate, the mystic wonder is inconceivable. Thus one is an assistant of heaven and earth. This is the highest level.

In the alchemy of spiritual power, heaven and earth are the crucible. The sun and moon are the medicinal ingredients. Spirit, energy, and vitality are culling and ingesting the elixir. Exhalation and inhalation are extraction and addition. The inner circulation of energy through the psychic channels is the firing process. This is the path of spiritual immortals. It is not easy to fulfill. One year is concentrated into one month, and it takes ten years to cultivate. When you use it all your life, you transcend the realms of desire, form, and formlessness, and become the same as heaven. If its highest attainment is consummated, three thousand practices are fulfilled and one becomes a spiritual immortal able to liberate people. In the middling grade there are eight hundred lofty achievements, and one becomes a flying wizard able to rescue people. In the lower echelon, one gathers medicine that boosts and enhances, and becomes a celestial wizard able to bring one's whole family to heaven. This is the second level.

In the alchemy of preserving unity, truthfulness is the crucible. Works are the medicinal ingredients.

Humanity and duty are the firing process. Chronicles and history are culling and ingesting the elixir. Speech and action are extraction and addition. This is the path of the lower adepts. The method is easy to practice, but hard to perfect. Ten years are concentrated into one day, and it takes one hundred years to cultivate to completion. The higher echelons forget themselves for the public welfare and are deputies of heaven. The lower echelons include the benefit of others in what they do for themselves and are lesser functionaries of heaven. The very lowest ones ingest herbs for long life and become earthly wizards. These are the lowest of the three levels, the dregs of the path of immortality.

Those on the foremost level leave being and enter nonbeing and are unfathomable, not trapped by life or death. Those on the second level can transform and die at will. They plunge into the origin, embrace the pristine, free the spirit, leave the body, and disappear from the world. They have birth but not death. Those on the third level work hard and accumulate achievement, becoming immortal after death. Even if they live a long time, it is not more than five hundred years.

Walk Slowly

Walk slowly, at a relaxed pace, and you won't stumble. Sleep soundly and you won't fret through the night. Practitioners first of all need serenity and patience. Second, they need dispassion, not to think about the past or be concerned about the future. If you think about the past, your former self will not die. If you think about the future, the road seems long and hard to traverse. It is better to be serene and relaxed, not thinking of past or future but just paying attention to the present, acting normally. Each accomplishment is an achievement, and this will build up. If you are eager for completion and vow to do so many deeds or practices, this is still personal interest, calculating merit and striving for gain. Then the mind cannot be pure. This is the root of inconsistency.

NOTES ON SOURCES

A more extensive selection of translations from Taoist writings is available in my *Vitality, Energy, Spirit: A Taoist Sourcebook* (Shambhala Publications, 1991).

My complete annotated translation of the *Tao-te Ching* and the "Inner Chapters" of *Chuang-tzu* are to be found in *The Essential Tao* (HarperCollins, 1991). My abridged translation of *Huai-nan-tzu* is to be found in *The Book of Leadership and Strategy: Lessons of the Chinese Masters* (Shambhala Publications, 1992).

The selections from the "Tales of Inner Meaning" have been taken from the following sources, with added material from oral tradition: *Zhongxi shide shenjing, Xianzhuanshiyi,* and *Gaodaozhuan.*

The selection of sayings attributed to Ancestor Lü has been taken from *Luzu huiji* and *Yulu daguan.*

BOOKS ON TAOISM BY THOMAS CLEARY

Tao Te Ching: Zen Teachings on the Taoist Classic (2010)*
Alchemists, Mediums & Magicians (2008)*
Taoist Classics: The Collected Translations of Thomas Cleary,
    4 vols. (2003)*
The Book of Balance and Harmony: A Taoist Handbook (2003)*
Taoist Meditation: Methods for Cultivating a Healthy Mind and
    Body (2000)*
Ways of Warriors, Codes of Kings: Lessons in Leadership from
    the Chinese Classics (2000)*
Sex, Health, and Long Life: Manuals of Taoist Practice (1999)*
Practical Taoism (1996)*
The Tao of Organization: The I Ching for Group Dynamics,
    by Cheng Yi (1995)*
Thunder in the Sky: Secrets on the Acquisition and Exercise of
    Power (1993)*
The Book of Leadership and Strategy: Lessons of the Chinese
    Masters (1992)*
Wen-tzu: Understanding the Mysteries, by Lao-tzu (1992)*
The Essential Tao (1992)
The Secret of the Golden Flower (1991)
Vitality, Energy, Spirit: A Taoist Sourcebook (1991)*
Back to Beginnings: Reflections on the Tao (1990)*
Mastering the Art of War, by Zhuge Liang & Liu Ji (1989)*
The Art of War, by Sun Tzu (1988)*

List continued on next page

Awakening to the Tao, by Liu I-ming (1988)*
The Buddhist I Ching, by Chihhsu Ou-i (1987)*
The Inner Teachings of Taoism, by Chang Po-tuan (1986)*
The Taoist I Ching, by Liu I-ming (1986)*

*Published by Shambhala Publications